OUTLINE OF BUSINESS

PART I

POCKET LIBRARY OF THE
WORLD'S ESSENTIAL KNOWLEDGE

VOLUME IX

OUTLINE OF BUSINESS
PART I

By GEORGE ROWLAND COLLINS,
M.A., M.B.A.

PROFESSOR OF MARKETING AND ASSISTANT DEAN OF THE
SCHOOL OF COMMERCE, ACCOUNTS, AND FINANCE,
NEW YORK UNIVERSITY

FUNK & WAGNALLS COMPANY
NEW YORK *and* LONDON

CONTENTS

THE OUTLINE OF BUSINESS—PART I

FOR NOTES TO CHAPTERS SEE END OF VOL. X

OUTLINE
OF BUSINESS

PART I

I

THE MEANING OF BUSINESS ECONOMY

In a panoramic sketch of machines and
merchandise, counting-houses and factories, in a
story of the evolution of the market-place, in an
exposition of current business organization, in
a scrutiny of accepted business technique, in any
speculation about the destiny of modern business, what can there be of cultural value to man
in civilization? What place has a knowledge and
understanding of "business" in the cultural
equipment of the average man?

Certain it is, that the intelligentsia who write
and talk for a living, and do little else, have long
been prone to castigate business. The sophisti-
cated and the cynical continually remind us that
business has contributed nothing to our civilization but crass materialism and the many and
varied debasements incident to its pursuit. Their
jottings are often intriguing. Some writers, like
Aldous Huxley, for example, are positive prophets of doom. In his recently published book,

Proper Studies, this younger Huxley decries business with the fervor of a professional crusader tilting at a devil technique. He says, in part:

> The qualities required of the contemporary servants of society are simply business acumen and the indispensable minimum of conventional honesty. Modern business organizers . . . fill their advertisements with sanctimonious phrases. For the benefit of their employees they publish grandiloquent accounts of the Firm's activities (The Firm or House is always spelt with a capital letter, as tho it were a divine entity), showing how efficiently and with what Christian devotion it serves the world. They train their children up in the belief that business is a religion.
>
> Success—"the bitch goddess, Success," in William James's phrase—demands strange sacrifices from those who worship her. . . . One thing alone is absolutely certain of the future: that our Western societies will not long persist in their present state. Mad ideals and a lunatic philosophy of life are not the best guarantees of survival.[1]

And yet, "business" is the work of the world, humanity's chiefest task. It has been so to a greater or lesser degree for centuries. Business Economy is with us to-day, and it is not likely to disappear ere the morrow. Entirely apart from the minutely particularized phases of business activity in which most of us are engaged, "business" touches our lives at a myriad points. We cannot escape its influence by sitting on the sidelines and watching the world plunge by. Its reach extends into our holiest cloisters and our most easeful retreats. Any attempt to flee it or to dismiss an understanding of it as unworthy of a place in our cultural equipment can only result in the extreme pessimism of some artificial philosophy of escape. Cynical despair is the invariable reaction of the man who will not make any emotional adjustment to an economic world that may be irrelevant to his dream. Then, too, it is hardly courageous either merely to lean back in skeptical observation of the passing scene or to shrink from the realism of the present in order to turn our faces back to the traditional glories of former ages.

To assert that our current business economy is all wrong is to assume not only that we ourselves are all fools but that our forbears, too, were all fools. For business economy as we have it was their work as much as it is ours. It is in part an unconscious growth from their innate tendencies and habits as human beings, and in part the conscious adaptation of that growth, by lopping and pruning and grafting to ends deemed desirable. The task of the present is for all to understand our current issue of business economy and its background growth in order to ascertain within what limits further

conscious lopping, pruning, and grafting may
be desirable.

A knowledge and understanding of business
economy is a necessary part of the cultural
equipment of every well-informed person, no
matter how active or inactive his or her part
may be in the actual guidance or conscious
adaptation of business economy. Such knowledge
and understanding is culturally important because business economy for centuries has constituted the substructure of civilization. The
arts, religion, and learning are, perhaps, the
finer aspects of civilization; but civilization is
many-sided. It involves economic considerations
as well as moral, spiritual, political, and esthetic
considerations. Apparently, the clearest and most
accurate definition of civilization is to be found
in the following sentence from the writings of
Mr. Charles A. Beard:

> Aside from all philological subtleties, civiliza-
> tion in its strict modern sense includes all these
> implements, devices, and practises by which men
> and women lift themselves above savages—the
> whole economic order, the system of leisure built
> upon it, the employment of that leisure, and all
> manifestations of religion, beauty, and apprecia-
> tion.[2]

The economic order is the material fabric of
civilization, the woven texture of the foundation
threads that free mankind from the status of the

savage. The arts, religion, and learning, of and by themselves, cannot make up the habiliments of civilization. Civilization's brightly decorated segments will survive only in so far as the material texture of her garment persists. As Mr. Beard has frequently pointed out, except for some of the minor decorative arts, a civilization cannot be borrowed without reproducing the accompanying economic order. The arts, religion, and learning, to be sure, are elements by which men and women lift themselves above the savage, but they are elements that are themselves bent to the economic order in which they live and thrive, that "have meaning and vitality only in relation to their economic substructure."[3]

The characteristic economic order of the present so-called western civilizations and of most preceding civilizations is a business or money-profits economy. The effects of this seeming dominance of civilization by a business or money-profits economy have been of incalculable importance. It was in a business economy that capitalistic methods were introduced into agriculture and into manufacturing. It was in a business economy that the commercial middle class induced the legal and constitutional revolutions of the eighteenth century under whose forms we still live. It was in a business economy that the machine was born and reared.

OUTLINE OF BUSINESS

Engines did not come to save men the brutality
of dull labor, to help an emperor build an imperial city, to irrigate and replenish waste lands
—they came because English traders wanted to
increase their profits by making cheaper cotton
to sell abroad.⁴

Indeed, one might ask the very pertinent question, What would have become of the celebrated
names in painting, poetry, sculpture, and architecture down through the centuries, had it not
been for the patronage and endowment of merchant princes, earning and profiting under an
order of business economy? The Medici in their
Florentine palaces had their Michelangelos,
Raphaels and Cellinis in generous number because they had the merchant earnings to call
forth great art. In the town of the thirteenth
and fourteenth centuries the humblest peasant
singer of rural ballads could always find a
merchant patron who would support and encourage him. In our present highly complex system
of business economy the money for learning and
the arts comes in increasing proportions from
taxes on business and gifts by captains of capi-
talism. And yet only the prophets of doom rise
up to say that the arts are languishing—architecture, painting, sculpture, music, literature,
design, and even the theater. Truly, while at
times the effects of "business" have been sordid
and venal, yet by and large business economy

[12]

is "a vehicle for the progress of humanity in all directions," the very means of existence for the finer aspects of civilization.

What is this economic system or order which we have called "business economy"? Many people become quite unnecessarily alarmed when they hear or read such terms as "political economy," "business economy," "profits economy," and so on. They think of economics as something dismal and of its terminology as too difficult for ordinary minds—like the Differential Calculus or the Fourth Dimension. As a matter of fact these terms are anything but difficult. "Economy" means simply: practical and systematic management. Coupled with the word "business" its meaning grows somewhat, but essentially the whole term "business economy" means nothing but practical and systematic management in making and spending money. The outstanding feature of an economic order which may be called a business economy is that economic activities are carried on mainly by making and spending money. A business economy does not develop in a geographical or political locality until most of the material activities of that locality take the form of making and spending money. When men, instead of making goods which their families need, "make" money, and with their money-incomes buy for their own use goods made by other hands, then dawns a business economy.

The mere use of money as a medium of exchange should not be mistaken as the matter of most importance to an understanding of the term "business economy." In Shakespeare's day, English standard money consisted mostly of silver coins. There were no copper coins and few gold coins. Shakespeare, then, rarely saw any except silver coins. Accordingly, he makes Bassanio as he determines his choice of caskets in *The Merchant of Venice* pass over the silver casket and address the metal in scorn as: "Thou pale and common drudge 'tween man and man." Money, in the sense of exchange, is just that: a drudge 'tween man and man. It is a tool with which to move commodities, a drudge that does a certain work—namely, that of passing goods from one man to another. The appearance and use of money as a convenient and widely-accepted tool of exchange in a community is not a significant consideration (altho a necessary one) in defining the economic order of that community as a business economy. The paramount matter is the organization of production, distribution, and consumption on a basis of money-making and money-spending.

A satisfactory definition of "business economy" is, then, as follows: A business economy is an institutional arrangement in which the

material activities of people consist of making
and spending money-incomes.[5] Money occupies
the central position in a business economy because it is the medium in terms of which economic motives express themselves. In a business
economy the material comfort or misery of a
family, for example, depends more upon its ability to command an adequate money-income and
upon its pecuniary thrift, than upon its efficiency in making useful goods and its skill in
husbanding supplies.[6] Charles Dickens reveals
the process through the mouth of Mr. Micawber.
"My other piece of advice, Copperfield," said
Mr. Micawber, "you know. Annual income
twenty pounds, annual expenditure nineteen
nineteen six, result HAPPINESS. Annual income twenty pounds, annual expenditure twenty
pounds ought and six, result MISERY. The
blossom is blighted, the leaf is withered, the
God of day goes down upon the dreary scene,
and—and in short you are forever floored. As
I am!"

In a business economy the principal driving
motive is inevitably the desire for profits. The
material needs of man, conditioned as they are
by the institutions of business economy, by the
very organization of production, distribution,
and consumption, cause every individual's welfare to be regulated very largely by pecuniary
considerations. Because of the influence of these

institutions the primary economic interest of
every individual consists in making money. Making goods is only a means of making money-
profits. "A person's command over want-satisfying goods and services is determined not by
his usefulness to society or his virtues as a citizen, but by the amount of money at his command." [7] The hope of profit is the causal influence behind the production of goods. Production
is not for society but "for the market." Business leaders subordinate the making of goods
to the making of money. They are compelled so
to do by the system of business economy of which
we all are parts. If they fail to make their
profits they cannot go on making goods.

To be sure, railroad employees, for instance,
serve the public or they would not have their
jobs. But they do not seek their jobs primarily
to serve the public. Some of them may find a
joy in this service, but even these insist upon
being paid for it. The same is true of miners,
bricklayers, plumbers, carpenters, and most
statesmen and politicians. Even teachers, doctors, and ministers in many cases (one is
tempted to say most) do not accept the opportunity to serve as the chief reward of their
professions. All over the world now, as you
ponder these thoughts, men are at work for
you—planting the tea you will one day drink,
sowing the corn you will one day eat, shearing

the wool you will one day wear, curing the tobacco you will one day smoke, and so on indefinitely. These men do not do these things because of any direct affection for you. To begin with, they do not even know you. They do these things to serve themselves, to make a money-profit. You can do none of these things for yourself. Unless they are done for you and unless you have enough money-income to secure their results for your use and enjoyment, you will, in the short run, be with Mr. Micawber, "on the rocks."

Natural resources, mechanical equipment, skill, and scientific technique will always be, as they always have been, factors of vital importance under any form of economic organization and in any civilization. In a business economy, moreover, natural resources are not and will not be developed, mechanical equipment is not and will not be utilized, skill is not and will not be exercised, scientific discoveries are not and will not be applied, unless conditions are such as to promise or hold out the hope of money-profit.[8]

From a purely social point of view, the aim of productive economic activity is to create utilities which will satisfy human wants. Money-making is important to a society because of its bearing upon efficiency in production. Comfort and misery, socially considered, do not depend upon the aggregate of money-incomes received by the individuals that make up society, but upon the abundance of useful goods produced by the society. Here, then, is the challenging material conflict in a business economy, the absorbing anomaly which has baffled and perplexed the economists of the past and present. The contradictions are plain. In a business economy, society is well off in proportion to its efficiency in producing a current supply of the necessities, comforts, and amenities of life, but an individual member of the same society is well off in proportion to his efficiency in acquiring a money-income.

It is this melodramatic conflict of contradiction which so intrigues the critics of "business." They look to the past and tease their minds with the methods of the bazaar, *Caveat emptor* (Let the buyer beware!) ; they look to the present and see only a piling up of non-utilities and anti-utilities for the sake of profit. They hurry to the conclusion that in a business economy the bristling economic contradictions can never be resolved, compromised, or integrated; that "business" is inevitably anti-social. Then they anathematize and damn!

However, it is extremely easy to exaggerate the seriousness of this conflict between making goods and making money, between social and individual ends. It is disengaging to dispose of the business man as selfish and self-seeking with

never a thought for the task of satisfying human
wants. So considered, the business man need not
and does not put on the market any real utilities. Rather, because he can make more money
through making and selling non-utilities and
anti-utilities, his "business sense" continually
prompts him to such a course. Hence an anti-
social result. Unfortunately for the business
critic, such a chain of reasoning contains many
highly precarious assumptions. There is, first,
the assumption that the growth of a business
and its profits, in the long run, depend upon
making and selling inferior goods or goods that
may even be hurtful to society. This assumption
hides a persistent and uncomfortable question:
Can such goods be disposed of continually and
consistently in "the market" at a profit? There
is, in the second place, the assumption that the
results of business efforts in the making and
selling of goods for money-profits are cate-
gorically pro-social results or anti-social results.
Such an assumption misinterprets the word
"social," a word that admits of the comparative
degree. Individual business activities produce
results which may be more social or less social.
Each individual business effort does not necessarily bring about a result that is perfectly
anti-social or perfectly pro-social. Finally, in
the foregoing reasoning, there is a somewhat
similar classifying difficulty, the difficulty of

classifying goods as "utilities," "non-utilities," or "anti-utilities" with an exact precision which will be universally accepted. So much depends upon the prejudice or preference of the classifier. From Rousseau to Spengler, for example, many classifiers have lived and died who protested against the "machine" as an anti-utility, socially considered. Few honest servants of humanity have been so roundly cursed as the "locomotive," the innocent child of Stephenson.

Again, money-profits are not the only incentive to business activity. Various other motives —some of them are of a very high order—are continually operating as productive stimuli. They have a place in a business economy that many of the early economists and most of our modern lampooning *literati* fail to give them. Senior's [9] proposition that "every man desires to obtain additional wealth with as little sacrifice as possible" is not the sole and cardinal factor. It is anything but the ultimate proposition in business economy beyond "which reasoning cannot go." [10] As a matter of fact, reasoning must go infinitely further if it is to take an inventory of all the mainsprings of business activities. The picture of the business man who, in his greed, is either engaged in holding back goods and services from a needy society or is mainly interested in cramming non-utilities and anti-utilities into the collective gullet of a credu-

lous public is not a typical or recognizable de-
lineation. Too many modern business men accept and believe Mr. Carver's apt observation
that "they who follow the pig-trough philosophy of life can never enjoy the prosperity of
those who follow the work-bench philosophy of
life." [11] The essential fact is merely this: In a
business economy, the individual business man
is obliged to make profits his first aim—not his
highest aim, not his ultimate aim, not his most
cherished aim, but his first aim—for unless he
does so, he is in danger of eliminating himself
from the business world. "A successful business
man is much more than a calculating machine;
but . . . he is first of all a good enough calculating machine to keep his balance sheets out
of the red." [12]

Moreover, the business man who organizes a
business with the first aim of making money-
profits may serve society as well or better than
he would if his first aim were not what it is.
Henry Ford has made it possible for almost anyone to own an automobile. His is probably a
service to society, altho from this statement
many ascetics and flagellants will dissent. Mr.
Ford, however, accomplished this service—for
so it is considered by the main stream of society
—by first seeking money-profits. As he made
money-profits he created "more jobs for more
men" and enlarged his service. An incidental

[21]

but significant thing about his activities is that
his one great attempt to serve without money-
profits—the Peace Ship Project—was a humili-
ating failure. He did not get the boys out of the
trenches before Christmas. All around us at this
moment, farmers, weavers, blacksmiths, mechan-
ics, cooks, physicians, *et al.*, are busily occupied
in the performance of the countless functions
necessary to the creation of goods and the rendi-
tion of services which we commonly require.
These men do these things to serve themselves,
to secure money-profits, yet they also serve us.
In other words, in a business economy, society
is sane enough and cute enough so to organize
the self-regarding tendencies of man as to produce results that probably could not be bettered
very much at any given moment if men suddenly
became what biologically they are not likely to
become, completely unselfish and entirely al-
truistic.

Our inquiry into the nature and meaning of a
business economy is not yet complete. There are
two very definite economic institutions, characteristic of our business economy, which need to
be presented and discussed. We have not discussed them before because they are not the exclusive possessions of a business economy. They
could exist outside of a business economy. But
now, in order better to understand the meaning
of business economy, and in order further to

avoid exaggerating the gravity of the conflict between social and individual ends in it, we must give some attention and thought to two important economic institutions, "private property" and "freedom of enterprise."

It seems impossible to conceive of "business" without the economic institution (established social habit) of the private ownership of property. The tobacco in the humidor by my side is my property. It is a commodity about to satisfy a want. When I feel the desire for a soothing smoke, I must be able to control the tobacco, the want-satisfying commodity. If someone could snatch and steal my tobacco at any time with impunity, wo betide my want, and my work as well, I fear. And when I say "impunity," I do not mean to indicate that my power to dispose of my tobacco (property) in the satisfaction of my want depends entirely upon the strength of my right arm. There was an age when man's power over his possessions was so dependent. But now the law protects me in my right of property: the law is my right arm. So long as man must defend his possessions with his right arm there is no property; he has no right. When he can appeal to an umpire to protect him, then his possession is guaranteed; his possession is transformed into property. Now, the tobacco in my humidor is my property only because the tobacco fields in Connecticut

and Virginia are someone else's property. The
two rights of private ownership of property are,
in a sense, linked together. If, in Virginia or in
Connecticut, the tobacco fields could be forcibly
seized by anyone who had the force, there would
soon be no fields of growing tobacco there and no
tobacco in my humidor. Business in this commodity would quickly cease. One of the most important economic institutions in a business economy, then, is the private ownership of property,
sanctioned and protected by society. This does
not mean that society has no claim on the property which it safeguards. Society has a claim
and exercises it through taxation, a claim which
is thoroughly and rigorously pressed. It does
mean, however, that society, in its own interests,
after it has stated and exacted its own claims,
must see that the balance which it does not
claim is carefully safeguarded for its owner.

Again, the tobacco is in my humidor because
anyone who likes is free to become a supplier
of tobacco and to offer to serve me, a con-
sumer of tobacco. In fact, many, many men, of
their own free will, have undertaken to become
vendors of tobacco. It so happens that I have
selected the one on a near-by corner to serve
my turn. At any time, if I do not like the way
he keeps my favorite brand in his cupboard
humidors, I am at liberty to walk across the
street and make my purchases elsewhere. I

can compel him to compete with his fellow retailers for my custom. In other words, this freedom of making, selling, and spending arises from property rights and is the privilege or right of doing what you want with what belongs to you. This does not mean, however, that society permits us unlimited freedom to exercise this right when its use endangers the safety, health, or moral welfare of others, or injures the general and common welfare.

The private ownership of property and freedom in the use of property have been accepted institutions of business economy for a very considerable period. They have been safeguarded purposively in our business economy and not out of malice. Even Sidney and Beatrice Webb, the distinguished exponents of social reform, do not hesitate so to testify:

> The economic institutions necessary to the vocation of profit-making—private property in the instruments of production, and free enterprise in the use of such instruments—were maintained and developed by British and American statesmen and legislators during the eighteenth and nineteenth centuries, with the approval of the economists, because these men honestly believed that unrestricted profit-making by manufacturers, traders, and financiers was the most effective way of increasing the national wealth.[13]

If we tone down the adjective ''unrestricted,'' it is safe to say that this statement represents

quite accurately the beliefs of a majority of the
leaders of business, the economists, and the
statesmen of the present day. Inevitably, of
course, there will always be some critics who will
speak and write of the institution of property
as tho it were "some piece of mechanism invented, manufactured, and forced upon an un-
willing people." [14] So, too, swayed by the old
proverb that "what is one man's meat is another man's poison," many will rise up to de-
nounce freedom of competition as contrary to
the whole spirit of ethics and religion which is
expressed in the Golden Rule—as a satanic
canker in our economic world.

Now, the confusion and conflict between social
and individual ends, which has been pointed out
as a striking economic anomaly in our business
economy, is caused, fundamentally, by these two
basic economic institutions, the right of private
ownership of property, and its derivative right
of freedom of enterprise.

"Private property" has been the central position against which the social movement of the last
hundred years has directed its forces. The criticism of it has ranged from an imaginative com-
munism in the most elementary and personal
of necessaries, to prosaic and partially realized
proposals to transfer certain kinds of property
from private to public ownership, or to limit
their exploitation by restrictions imposed by the
State. But, however varying in emphasis and in

method, the general note of what may conveniently be called the Socialist criticism of property is what the word Socialism itself implies. Its essence is the statement that the economic evils of society are primarily due to unregulated operation, under modern conditions of industrial organization, of the institution of private property.[15]

The only way completely to resolve the economic conflict, to establish a situation in which the interests of every individual would be entirely compatible with the interests of the group, would be to scrap "private property" and its twin, "freedom of enterprise." A mere reversion to a barter economy—the exchange of goods without the use of money—would not resolve the economic anomaly. The same friction between social and individual ends would persist in a system of barter if "private property" and "freedom of enterprise" remained as essential economic institutions. The important point is here: a business or money-profits economy does not cause the economic anomaly, the conflict between social and individual ends. The most that can be said is, that a business or money-profits economy may intensify the conflict.

And yet the business economy of the present in all probability leads to the creation of greater wealth and promotes the common welfare better than any other feasible economic system that has ever been tried on a large scale or that has yet been devised and suggested by the minds of men. To date, production and distribution on a large scale and embracing a sufficient variety of goods to satisfy consumers has nowhere been successful except under the urge of the profit motive of a business economy.[16] Moreover, our present business economy has evolved through a process of human selection. As Mr. W. C. Mitchell has pointed out, our present business or money-profits economy has developed spontaneously in all the most progressive nations of the world.[17] When some pioneer first decided to spend all his time making shoes, he was obliged to secure his food from someone else. He was not forced to spend all his time making shoes, but he decided that he would be better off by so doing than if he also produced his own food. He sold his shoes for a money-profit and bought his food by paying a money-profit to the producer of food. It was an arrangement that benefited both.

No one forced our forefathers in America to give up raising their own food, making their own clothing, and cutting their own fuel. They changed from the practise of making goods for their own families to the practise of making money-incomes and buying goods made by others because they liked the results of the more elaborate plan better. . . . So almost all the elaborate machinery of the money-economy has grown up by slow degrees because men thought they got

more goods or better goods when they worked
for money than when they produced for themselves.[18]

Such, then, in broad outline, is the meaning
of business economy. The picture, of course, is
not completely developed and finished. It needs
some background detail touching upon the Evolution of Business Economy, some vivid description of the Modern Organization for Making
Money, some clear exposition of the Technique
of Modern Business Activities, and some careful
analysis and sober consideration of Present and
Future Business Problems. These details the
following chapters will attempt to present.

Throughout the succeeding pages, in order to
combat the cynical distrust and despair of the
critics of "business," it will not be necessary to
assume that our present business economy is
working perfectly or that there are no evils
growing out of it. If such an assumption were
possible "there would be nothing more to be
done except to enjoy the economic Eden to which
our portion of the human race had been restored." [19] Certainly such perfection has not
yet been attained. The important considerations
are simply these:

1. Does our present business economy contain
   possibilities of conscious adaptation and improvement that will bring us to some solution
   of the so-called economic anomaly?

2. If so, are we making progress in that direction?
3. Can we retain the good and extract the evil from our characteristic economic institutions without scrapping our business economy in its entirety and starting over with some entirely new system or economic order?

Broadly speaking, there are three ways of dealing with conflict: resolution, compromise, or integration. Which method shall we adopt in dealing with the economic anomaly? This question, our survey of the Evolution of Business Economy, our description of the Modern Organization for Making Money, our exposition of the Technique of Modern Business Activities, and our analysis of the Problems of the Future, will attempt to answer.

II

THE ANCIENT BEGINNINGS

SOME sense of the history of "getting and spending" as the common adventure of most of mankind is necessary to any sure understanding of our present business or profits economy. In fact, even a casual speculation concerning any of the institutions of our contemporary civilization—political, social, religious, esthetic, or economic—leads us back to England and France, to Germany and Italy, to Rome and Greece and Palestine and Persia and Egypt. Unfortunately, it is a common convention for writers and orators to assume that any serious thesis or platform speech must begin with Babylon, Greece, and Rome, a convention which is ofttimes boring to the yawning point. Worn-out chronicles and non-essential preliminaries kill interest. However, the tale of the evolution of present-day "business" is presented here not because it is conventional so to proceed, but because the history of business economy—its genesis and exodus, its wanderings, and its sight of the promised land—is logically necessary. We cannot fairly forswear the past.

Nomads of the desert, dwellers in Athens and Alexandria, hunting tribes in the European for-

ests, fishermen of the North Sea; the worlds
of the Persians and the Hebrews, of the Greeks
and the Romans, of the Arabs and the Christians
and the Jews, of Italian and German merchants,
of French and English peasants—all these have
given ideas and ways of living to modern
America. Take away one of these ages and peoples, and our own civilization would be the
poorer. All have played their part in giving us
our culture.[1]

Mankind has always been an incessant bor-
rower. Man's sole originality has always lain in
the new combinations of old ideas and institutions which he has been forced to make. The
basic and unit elements that form the economic
substructure of our contemporary civilization
are recorded in the annals and log-books of a
dozen different ages and peoples. Because our
present business or profits economy is the "heir
of many ages" and is scarred by the conflicts of
its own evolution, because it has been "woven
from a host of different elements," each one of
which has left its impress, it is impossible to
comprehend the economy of the present without
knowing the record of its past.

Moreover, it should be said again that the
material institutions of an economic order are
causal elements which mold all the finer aspects
of a civilization. It is not putting the cart before the horse to say that civilization, in a
narrowly esthetic meaning, is a creature of eco-

nomic circumstance. The economic order bends and twists the arts, religion, and learning to its own purposes. The institutional structure of the economic order under which a civilization lives fashions the "finer" aspects of that civilization. And the "finer" aspects have "meaning and vitality only in relation to their economic substructure." Purely "cultural" traces of previous orders persist and push themselves upward to be borrowed and worked into new combinations by new orders, "but they thrive only in so far as they carry with them the soil that originally nourished them." [2] In this generation these propositions are becoming widely accepted and the necessity for an economic interpretation of all history is bearing in upon the minds of our most academic historians, purists in political, social, religious, or esthetic history tho they may be. Some systematized knowledge of the evolution of the present business or profits economy, then, seems worthwhile and pertinent to the average man in order that he may clarify his notions about "business" and its contributions to preceding civilizations and to our own. So equipped, he will be better able to invite those who with cynical facility decry "business," in all its aspects and in its entire history, to deliver a bill of particulars.

From still another point of view, an orderly survey of the development of business economy is important. To the humble observer who looks out of his window at the daily stream of "business," inquiring its course, the phenomenon appears as a commonplace and organic whole. It seems to defy any division and examination of its component parts. The simple fact is that we are all so close to contemporary "business" that it is well-nigh impossible for us to view it objectively. The best we can do is to practise a kind of subjective "introspection into our own mental processes" as they relate to business activities. Unless we detach ourselves from the present to peer into the past, an objective vista is almost unattainable. Our best procedure, then, in any effort to comprehend the present is to trace the whole growth and development of the uses of money in the economic order. Only by filling in our background objectively can we hope to analyze the contemporary situation. Only by maintaining a proper perspective of the past and by noting how mankind "has slowly evolved one element in the complex after another," will that which is "so familiar and organic a whole to us" dissolve "into thought-suggesting parts."

Three methods of presenting the tale of "business" are available. We may proceed chronologically by following the sequence of the years, or we may discuss business development stage-by-stage without particular reference to

time, or we may do both. In order to provide a
sufficient background, it seems wise to use the
last-named method. Accordingly, the balance of
this chapter and the two chapters which follow
will attempt to sketch the evolution of our contemporary business economy by following the
order of passing time, by relating events to se-
quential dates. The "whens" are significant.
Every important happening has causes and results, and to discover these causes and results
we must know what preceded and followed the
particular happening.

An economic order at any time consists of
specific events, customs, and institutions, that
go together. What unites them is their simul-
taneous occurrence. "They are a bundle of sticks
which must be tied together with a date." [3] In
order to associate closely together all simultane-
ous happenings and to cultivate a feeling of perspective for the lapse of time, some familiarity
with a chronological survey of business economy
is highly desirable. But this familiarity alone
will not suffice. In a sense, any division of the
historical stream into such parts or periods as
ancient, medieval, and modern is fundamentally fallacious. [4]

The status of an economic order is not determined absolutely by the element of time. In
fact, from the point of view of time, the development of business economy has not been at all

uniform over the whole of this earthly globe or over all the sections of any country on it. In this twentieth century, business economy exists in some areas in a stage of infancy. In others it is adolescent and in still others it is mature. The time sequence is immaterial in the purely genetic sense of an evolution from the simple to the complex. The distinction involved in a classification of business economies as ancient, medieval, and modern, considered as simple products of time, is without much meaning.[5] What is important is the stage-by-stage development of business economy. Consequently, in order to complete the background, the final chapter of this part of our study attempts a descriptive survey of the general stages of economic development.

The chronological history of economy harks back through the ages and into the haze that hides the beginning of humanity. In the far-off, dim stretches of time, men began to take their faltering first steps toward the use of money. Of this vague and remote past we have few certain records and so in our school-days this whole period was commonly called prehistoric—beyond the bounds of history. To-day, because of the discoveries of the archeologists and the anthropologists, some historians are loath to use the adjective "prehistoric" and venture many inferences about these systematically-unrecorded ages.

THE ANCIENT BEGINNINGS

And yet, in spite of the valuable material discoveries of the archeologists and the careful measurements, classifications, and generalizations of the anthropologists, our knowledge of these dim days is so scanty and meager and is so loosely tied together by conjecture and guesswork that it is far from reliable.

The story of the past as it has reached us is, indeed, in many respects like the ruin of some ancient amphitheater or medieval monastery. Some sections are better preserved than others, some parts are gone entirely, others have been faultily restored by later writers who failed to catch the spirit of the original. In some places nothing is left but a shapeless core of vague statements or a few bare dates and facts. Elsewhere we get a vivid glimpse of the life of the past in its original coloring. Sometimes the story has improved with age, as ruins are sometimes beautified by becoming weather-beaten or overgrown with moss. So the haze of romance, or the glamour of hero-worship, or the mere spell of antiquity, add to the past a charm that is history's own.[6]

The evolution of economy in the so-called prehistoric period was probably a very slow and tedious development. Conjecture has it that man first began to exchange gifts and then to barter for the sake of goods. An animal fur may have been the first article ever bartered. A weapon for hunting, perhaps a stone club, may have been the next. Thus the modern fur dealer and sporting-goods merchant may perhaps lay claim to the greatest antiquity in "trade" as distinguished from "business." However that may be, it is certain that we cannot go back to the time when men did not barter—trade goods for goods. Amber, found only in the Baltic, was common in the earliest ages of Ancient Greece. And epochs before that, goods moved about the so-called prehistoric world in astounding fashion. Expert judges think that certain stone axes, discovered in France along with other relics of primitive man, are made of a kind of jade found only in far-off Asia.

Barter begins with the exchange of superfluous goods. A man with a weapon to spare, say a tomahawk, barters it for a bundle of cord for tying up the hair. Later, as life becomes settled, the separation of employments or the so-called "division of labor" begins. The man who is particularly skilled in making weapons finds that his products are in demand by others and gives more and more time to that in which he excels. He discovers that he can build up a surplus of weapons and barter that surplus for his living necessities. Then, in all probability, the concept of ownership begins to take more definite form. Then, too, begin experimental efforts to express values in a common denominator and to use some commodity as currency. These early attempts to develop specialized occupations, to hold markets, to find a medium of exchange, and to "mix trading as a business with cattle lifting, man stealing and town sacking" shroud the genesis of business economy.

Just when man began to use coined money is not definitely ascertainable. Before the sixth or seventh century B. C. practically all trade was carried on by barter—the exchange of goods for goods. It is quite unlikely that there was any credit or coined money.

> The ordinary standard of value with the early Aryans was cattle, as it still is with the Zulus and Kaffirs to-day. In the *Iliad,* the respective values of two shields are stated in head of cattle, and the Roman word for moneys, *pecunia,* is derived from *pecus,* cattle.[7]

Anything, of course, can be money that will do the money work, and a curious assortment of things have been used as money at one time or another—shells, sheep, iron ingots, blocks of salt, bullets, cubes of pressed tea, and so on. In the colonial days of our own country, tobacco was legal tender; in West Africa fines are paid and trades are made in the currency of gin. Aristotle tells us that iron supplied the first currency, and Cæsar in *De Bello Gallico* mentions the fact that iron bars of fixed weight were used for currency in Britain. "Leather money," the statement and seal of some established firm on "leather" (parchment) by which it promised to pay so much silver or gold, is probably as old as coinage, or older. Coins may have had their first inception as decorations for the body, the need for decoration being probably as urgent with primitive man as it is with naked savages and wealthy dames to-day. From value as a decoration to value as a tool of exchange would be but a short step. Units of coined money, however, were probably evolved almost directly from units of commodity money.

The natural products of a community are first used as money units. But commodity units are inconvenient. In the use of commodity units, there is, of course, the difficulty of "coincidence" of wants, that important drawback to barter—each party having a thing to dispose of, but neither being able to provide what the other wants. But there are other difficulties, too, in the use of commodity units. There is the difficulty of defining quantity and quality. No one sheep, no one slave is exactly the same as another. Commodity units are not conveniently homogeneous.[8] Metallic money, whether coined or not, because of its convenience, inevitably asserts itself sooner or later. At first, in all probability, the coined money in a particular place represents the article which has previously served as a commodity unit in that place.

Thus we have the tunny fish of Cyzicus, the silphium plant of Cyrene, indicating staple products, while the double ax of Tenedos, and the kettle of Creti, may not improbably be derived from manufactured articles for which the locality was highly celebrated.[9]

At the dawn of history, certainly, coined money was in full use. Abraham paid for the cave and field of Machpelah with "four hundred shekels of silver, current money with the merchants," money coined of the metal that formed the standard money of England until 1816. The most generally-accepted guess seems to be that the invention of money coinage—pieces of precious metal stamped and purporting to be of a certain weight—took place in Western Asia Minor, Lydia, about 600 B. C.[10] Coined money may have been used in Babylonia before that time, but in all likelihood early currency was confined to metal ingots which required weighing at each transaction. Gold coins were struck by the Phenicians about 330 B. C. and were thereafter carried and popularized by these hardy seafarers throughout the Mediterranean world.

In point of time, the Egyptians were the first people to build a highly-developed civilization. Modern scholars agree that at about 3000 B. C., when the pyramids, the most majestic monuments ever built by man, were raised to stand "immutable and eternal in the desert," Egyptian civilization reached an astonishingly high level. Moreover, it can be traced back many more thousands of years before Christ. The Egyptian civilization, however, was an agricultural rather than a commercial civilization, and its economy was mainly a barter economy rather than a money or business economy. True, the Egyptians developed some of the industrial arts to great efficiency. They were expert metallurgists in metals other than iron. They could "smelt them, draw them into wire, beat them into sheets, cast them into molds, emboss, chase, engrave, inlay, and enamel them." [11] They were expert woodworkers, skilled irrigation engineers, admirable sculptors and architects in stone, acceptable draftsmen and painters, and adept weavers. But they used most of the products of their highly developed industrial arts for direct consumption rather than for trade.

Because of the geographical position of the country as situated on the highway from the East to Europe, Egypt was eventually forced into commerce, and, beginning about 600 B. C., regular trading-communication was established with Asia. Caravans brought precious woods, ivory, gold, wine, and oil into Egypt from Phenicia, Syria, and the Red Sea district, and carried back grain, linen, weapons, rings, and chains. Before the eyes of Joseph and his brethern, "behold, a company of Ishmaelites came from Gilead with their camels bearing spicery and balm and myrrh, going to carry it down to Egypt.'' However, only in this last period of Egyptian independence, from about 600 B. C. to 332 B. C., when the country was conquered by Alexander, did ''commerce'' and ''trade'' flourish. In these years, ''the government, which formerly had discouraged trade, now permitted and encouraged it; Greek merchants came in considerable numbers to Egypt; and an active commerce sprang up.'' [12] Some, at least, of the characteristics of a business economy made their appearance late in this period. Contracts were entered into involving the future, rude accounts were kept, bills of exchange appeared, some Persian coins were circulated and exchanged for thirteen times their weight of silver, specialized merchandising ''criers'' (the ancestors of contemporary personal salesmen) sang out announcements of caravan and ship arrivals describing ''in florid language the regions from which the articles came and the difficulties under which they were obtained.'' [13] By and large, however, until its conquest, Egypt remained under a barter economy. The use of coined money was rare and was sharply confined to a limited number of traders. The fundamentals of business economy left untouched the economic position of the great mass of people.

In the valley of the twin rivers Tigris and Euphrates, too, there grew up in the days be-

yond written record an intermixture of peoples
whose economic activities are important to the
story of business economy. On the lower Euphrates, the great city of Babylon became a
center for a Semitic people. High up the Tigris,
a mixed people termed Assyrians established
the center of Nineveh. For many years reign-
ing power "swayed between Nineveh and
Babylon, and sometimes it was an Assyrian and
sometimes a Babylonian who claimed to be 'king
of the world,' " the world of Mesopotamia. In
point of time, ancient Babylonia rose to importance first, some centuries after 3000 B. C. Fortune frowned, and in 745 B. C. Babylonia became
subject to Assyria under Tiglath-Pileser II. Subject she remained until 625, when Nabopolassar
joined the Medes and destroyed the Assyrian
power. This later Babylonian Empire extended
to 539 B. C., when the independent kingdom fell
before the Persian sword. The Assyrians were
preeminently a warlike, the Babylonians a commercial and luxury-loving people, so that it is
the latter-named people that have a special interest for us.

The position of the city of Babylon on
the lower Euphrates, near the Persian Gulf,
made it a great market-place for the trade between India and eastern and western Asia with
the nearest parts of Africa and Europe. From
Ceylon came ivory, cinnamon and ebony; from

Arabia myrrh and frankincense; from the islands in the Persian Gulf cotton, pearls and valuable timber; from northern India gold, dyes, jewels and fine wool. The wealth of Babylon became enormous and proverbial in large measure because of her own ingenious and splendid manufactures. Carpets, curtains and fine muslins, skilfully woven and brilliantly dyed, of elegant pattern and varied hue, were famous wherever luxury existed. Clay was abundant and craftsmen developed extraordinary skill in the ceramic arts.

In this Babylonian civilization, we certainly have the very definite beginnings of a business economy. Barter was still the method of trade for many, but by the latter part of the second Babylonian Empire the use of silver as a standard of value in trade was widespread. The silver was melted into ingots, which were called after the weights to which they corresponded, the lightest current weight being the shekel, the medium weight the minæ, and the heaviest the talent.[14] Trade was well developed, and traders were classified. Different words were used for wholesaler and retailer. The former was a dealer who acted both as an exporter and as an importer. The latter was a dealer who made all his purchases from the wholesaler.

It is possible that the idea of interest first appeared in Babylonia, for the hiring of com-

mercial capital was practised at rates of twenty
per cent. or more. Written contracts, signed and
witnessed, were frequently drawn by public
scribes. The thumb-marks of the contracting
parties were imbedded in the clay before the
tablet contracts were baked in a public oven,
so that falsification or forgery was almost impossible. Accounts were also inscribed and
baked on clay tablets or bricks which were
"proof against fire or the ravages of time."
Since these tablets or bricks permitted of various methods of orderly arrangement, we may say
that the Babylonians were the inventors of the
contemporary loose-leaf ledger and the card-
index system of accounts.[15] The uncovered tablet-
accounts of the Murashu Sons of Nippur present a fifty-year record (about 400-350 B. C.) of
such business transactions as the leasing of
canals, lands, and animals, the securing of the
rights of irrigation, and the payment of taxes.[16]
The Babylonian business transactions were many
and varied, and expressed in their records the
essence of much of the later commercial law.
One writer on ancient law goes so far as to
assert that there is "no legal conception or legal
transaction of the Roman law at the height of its
development that does not find its counterpart
in Babylon."[17]

However advanced the Babylonian civilization
may have been in the sense of a developing busi-

ness economy, if we seek in ancient times a people whose very existence depended upon making a business of "trade" and "commerce" we must look further. The Semitic merchants and seafaring folk who dwelt in the Phenician cities of Tyre, Sidon, Byblus, Berytus, Tripolis, and Ptolemais were the most thoroughly active commercial people of ancient times. Tyre was a powerful city as early as 1200 B. C., and long before the Greeks and the Romans arose upon the world's stage Phenician mariners were masters of the Mediterannean. What the Hebrew prophet Ezekiel sagely said of Tyre might have been said of all the Phenician cities: "Thou that dwellest at the entry of the sea, that art the merchant of the people unto many isles. . . . Thy borders are in the heart of the seas."

> At the end of the Mediterranean Sea, half-way between the East and the West, to each of which Phenicia stretched out in trade; within easy reach of Egypt, Arabia, and Armenia; protected against destructive invasions by the Lebanon Mountains at her back; invited to navigation by the sea at her feet; and well supplied with timber for ships, this land enjoyed in her position a greater *geographical advantage* than did any other country of antiquity.[13]

It is little wonder that from the eleventh to the sixth centuries B. C., the trade of Tyre and of her sister-cities reached almost throughout the then-known world. These oft-called "pedlers of antiquity" exported wares and manufactures of their own; they imported and reexported products of every region east and south of their own land, products that had any value for the markets of the nations dwelling round the great central sea. So to Phenicia came the spices of Arabia; the ivory, ebony and cotton goods of India; linen-yarn and corn from Egypt; wool and wine from Damascus; embroideries from Babylon and Nineveh; horses and chariots from Armenia; copper from the shores of the Euxine Sea; lead and silver from Spain; tin from Cornwall. From Phenicia there went to foreign ports, not only these articles of food and of luxury, but the rich purple dyes made from the murex (a kind of shell-fish) of the Phenician coast, the famous hue of Tyre, with which were tinged the costly silken robes worn by ancient despots. From Sidon went the not less famous glass produced in part from fine white sand found near the headland called Mount Carmel. Gold, silver, bronze, and iron were known to the artisans and were worked. The Phenician drinking-cups of silver and of gold, the bracelets and necklaces of Tyre, and Sidon's works in brass were famous. Great as the Phenician workers were at the dyeing vat and loom, in working metals and in fabricating glass, they were also accomplished miners and the most skilled ship designers and

[48]

builders in all early history. As mariners their renown was more lasting then their "trade" or "commerce," for their ships saw service either as mercenaries or in payment of tribute in the fleets of other countries, and Phenician "lessons in seamanship" long outlived the commercial prominence of her cities.

The Phenicians were the earliest people to inaugurate and execute a systematic plan of colonization. They established garrisoned trading posts in favored positions at the mouths of rivers, on islands, peninsulas, and projecting headlands —in Cyprus, on the islands of the Ægean Sea, on the northern coast of Africa, in Sicily, and in Spain. The extent of their colonization was indeed remarkable. The endurance of colonial allegiance, however, was limited, for the colonies were held to the motherland by nothing but a commercial bond. Phenicia herself was but a series of cities, each with an independent government, so that she forced no political bonds upon her colonies. By far the most renowned of all Phenician colonies—famous in poetry for Dido's hapless love and hapless death, in history for Hannibal's heroic hate of Rome and warlike skill—was Carthage, established in the center of the northern coast of Africa about 850 B. C. and destined by 500 B. C. to incorporate the cities of Phenicia and the colonies of the West into the commercial Carthaginian State.

Among such a people we should certainly expect to find many of the institutions and much of the technique of an infant business economy. But such expectations have a disappointing basis in the available written record. Phenicia was so essentially commercial that she neglected letters, and as a result we are dependent upon her enemies for her history. It is reasonably certain that during the period of the greatest Phenician prosperity a barter economy completely prevailed. The caravans and the ships carried goods of small value in one region to another land where they were highly prized, and goods acquired in exchange were taken to still other places where they were valued highly. "Incredible profits" were made by repeated exchanges of goods for goods. Gold coins, as has been stated, were not struck by the Phenicians until 330 B. C., long after the decline of the commercial supremacy of Tyre and Sidon. The use of coined money in exchange was popularized by the Phenician sailors, but not until Phenician ascendancy gave way to that of Carthage. To what extent the Phenicians accepted and protected the institution of "private property" by law, to what extent they used bills of exchange, to what extent they kept accounts, to what extent they carried on banking transactions—all these are matters of conjecture. Most historians are inclined to depict these "missionaries of

civilization" as imitators, borrowers, and dis-
seminators. If this picture is accurate, the Phenicians were mere adapters and teachers of the
trading techniques evolved in other lands by
preceding and contemporary peoples. At all
events, and in spite of the preoccupation with
"commerce" and "trade" of the majority of the
population, the available record does not indicate the existence of a strict business economy
in Phenicia.

Like Phenicia, Carthage was essentially a
"trading" and maritime state. Like Phenicia,
Carthage left few records that are valuable to
the history of business economy. Like Phenicia,
Carthage supported herself by the trade and
tribute of an extensive colonial empire. Unlike
Phenicia, however, Carthage enforced her power
upon her colonies and aggressively exploited
them. In the city itself, manufacturing seems to
have been sharply limited. There was, instead,
a lively interest in the agricultural possibilities
of northern Africa, and farming was "in high
favor and was engaged in by all classes." What
is probably the earliest formal treatise on farming is one of the few pieces of Carthaginian
writing that have been preserved. In the later
period of Carthaginian ascendancy there appears to have been a widespread use of credit
currency in the form of "leather money," not
only among the specialized traders, but among

the majority of the city's population. This "leather money" seems to have consisted of almost any material, the size and shape of a coin, wrapped in leather and sealed and stamped by the government.[19] It circulated on the credit of the government, and people reckoned their wealth in it.[20] In this connection it should be stated that fabricating various forms of leather and making many kinds of stamped and embossed leather articles was Carthage's chief manufacturing interest.

By 300 B. C., bills of exchange and letters of credit apparently were in use, and evidently a certain amount of lending on ships as security was practised. As early as 450 B. C. the Carthaginians came into conflict with the Greek colonies. Some of the motley Carthaginian colonies refused tribute. Then came Rome and the Punic Wars. In 202 B. C., Carthage became a subject ally of Rome. Finally, in 146 B. C., Carthage's doom was pronounced when Rome decreed that the city should be destroyed and that any new city built within her territory should be located at least ten miles from the sea. "Carthage had been 'queen of the waters,' but her glory was ended by this Roman edict."[21]

Mention of the Greeks brings before us another people who were for a time the leading merchants of the great inland sea of antiquity. Peninsular Greece was a "land of shores." It

is said that no country in the world of an equal
area presents so many islands, bays, peninsulas,
and harbors. No point is more than a few miles
from the coast, and the land extends no farther
than the "sea breeze." Moreover, every island
in the Greek Sea is in plain sight either of the
mainland or of another island. It is little wonder that the sea and its influence are everywhere
observed in Grecian history. The Greeks regarded the sea as a "highway," and the islands
of the Ægean as "stepping stones" to navigation. Very early, then, probably about 1000
B. C., the Greeks became a maritime people. And
yet for some time they did not take advantage
of their opportunities and were content to leave
commerce and trading in the hands of the
Phenicians. Little by little, however, the Greeks
supplanted the Phenicians as Greek colonization
grew.

> The Greek colonies reached to nearly all the
> shores of the Mediterranean and its numerous
> branches. Cicero termed these settlements a "Greek
> fringe." The colonists did not go far inland, and
> everywhere they came in contact with the Pheni-
> cians, who had preceded them. In some cases
> their predecessors were expelled, in others the
> Greeks withdrew.[22]

This process of colonization continued until
about 600 B. C. and all the while the Greeks were
ready pupils of the Phenicians. Greek ship-

building progressed and Greek sailors gradually ousted the Phenicians as carriers of wares. At home the Greeks learned to practise agriculture, and the textile and metal manufactures. They began to produce goods for export, not only to the colonies but to other markets; they "emancipated themselves from their former dependence on Oriental manufactures and developed the clay, bronze, and woolen industries to a point not dreamed of before." [23]

For forty years, from 625 B. C. to 585 B. C., Corinth was undoubtedly the leading commercial city in Greece. Located on the narrow isthmus which controlled the passage by land to the Peloponnesus, Corinth was sometimes termed "the eye of Greece," or because of the harbor at each side of the peninsula with a low elevation between was called "the bridge of the seas." Here it was that light ships were dragged over the isthmus on rollers and that heavy ships "broke cargo" (unloaded their goods to be carried across and reshipped on the other side) in order that merchant sailors might avoid the dreaded voyage around the rocky tip of the Peloponnesus. Industrially, Corinth was active and carried on manufactures in leather, pottery, textiles, and metals. The bronze work of Corinth was especially notable and was exported over the ancient world.

From 585 B. C. to 400 B. C. Athens rose to first

place among the Greek cities and maintained its supremacy until subjugated by Macedonia under Philip about 338 B. C. Athenian merchant-navigators conducted a large carrying trade for other peoples. In fact, perhaps a majority of the exports were foreign wares which were merely transshipped in the Piræus, the Athenian port, which was connected with the city by walls. The native exports of Athens were silver and other metals from the mines near the city, metal wares manufactured from copper and bronze, pottery, and objects of art. The imports were grains, wine, oil, and spices, wool, leather, fish, and articles of luxury. Wheat, in fact, "was imported, stored and sold by the State; nominal prices only were charged for grain, and at times it was given away in what was termed the 'dole.'"

The Greeks were not primarily an industrial people. Manufacturing was sharply limited and confined to articles of fine esthetic craftsmanship. The Grecian philosophy of life found small place for industrial impulses. Labor was degraded. The artisan was less respected than the farmer. Aristotle's theories taught that leisure was the "mother of culture," and as a consequence the citizen who lived in idleness was often held in high regard. Slavery was an accepted economic institution, and the slaves made possible existent agriculture, manufacture and trade.

And yet while the Grecian civilization in its economic particulars was not primarily industrial and appears to have been commercial only in necessary degree, many of the elements of a business economy are recorded in it. In the early period, trade, of course, was carried on by barter. Shortly after 600 B. C., when the art of coinage was begun in Lydia, coinage was introduced into Greece, where it flourished in high perfection. The silver mines of Laurium supplied Athens with metal for coinage, and silver was used for the coins of high denomination. The commonest Greek coin was ultimately the silver *stater* (shekel) or *didrachmon* of 135 grains. Copper was used to some extent for coins of lower denominations, tho the Greek silver *drachma* of about 65 grains was also current. Gold was not common in Grecian coinage until the last of the fourth century B. C. The very earliest Greek coins were probably struck at Ægina and for purposes of foreign rather than of internal trade. Yet coins soon found their way into the transactions of ordinary life, and by the time of Solon (600 B. C.), "a money economy had almost superseded the natural economy of Homeric Greece." [24]

Two types of Grecian coinage developed—the Pheidonian coinage, which circulated in the south and west, and the Eubœan coinage, which became somewhat standard at Athens and was used chiefly in the central and eastern sections. This dissimilarity in coinage made bankers necessary. The early Grecian bankers were called "table merchants" because they carried on their money-changing and money-testing at a table. Later, they expanded their operations to include the custody of money and the lending of money. In Solon's time, bankers made advances of silver to farming peasants on the security of the debtor's land. Moreover, they shared in the profits of trading ventures by lending money on "bottomry," on the security of a given vessel or cargo, for the voyage out or back or both. Interest rates were excessive, sometimes as high as forty-eight per cent. on "bottomry," and creditors were relentless.[25] Indeed, much of Solon's celebrated legislation was directed against the money-lenders and was intended to relieve the suffering of debtor citizens.

As early as 600 B. C. there existed an ever-increasing group of wealthy capitalists. Private capital was employed in every direction.

At first sight it might seem as if the field for private enterprise was rather limited, since the collectivist ideal of State-ownership was realized in Athens to a considerable extent; the State was the proprietor of the land, the mines, the harbors, and most of the means of production. Still,

the actual conduct of business was closely parallel
to that with which we are familiar, since all
public undertakings were let out on stated payments for longer or shorter periods to capitalists,
who worked them for the time to their own
advantage. Thus, tho the resources of production
were not appropriated by private persons, they
were regularly administered by private capitalists who farmed them out. . . .

. . . Some of the operations which were thus
carried on by private capital were so large that
no individual could undertake them, and they
were let to partnerships or associations of moneyed men. Such were the companies which undertook the farming of the various taxes. The
collection of the harbor dues and the customs on
imports, as well as the taxes on resident aliens,
were all leased in this fashion.[26]

The principle of joint-stock association was apparently well understood by the Greeks, for it is
frequently mentioned in connection with ship-
owning, mining, and other commercial ventures.

Greek merchants were separated rather
sharply into the two common classes, wholesalers
and retailers. The wholesalers were the import-
ers and usually, too, the ship-owners. They
either commanded the ships themselves or com-
missioned others to command for them. The retailers were more true to the present-day type
of individual retailer in that they confined
"their operations to one city, and sold wares
either in small shops, or in the booths of the

market, which was a fixed institution in most
Greek cities.'' In the larger cities, special
markets for particular goods were fixed for
known spots and certain times. While locations
were definite, many retailers did not hesitate to
come out of their shops to hawk their goods
about the streets or to hire a public crier of
carrying voice.[27] Advertising in the form of shop
signboards was also in use. The merchandising
methods of *caveat emptor* (let the buyer beware)
were typical, for false weights and short-chang-
ing were common. Water was put into wine and
the poulterers blew air under the skin of the
fowls to make them appear fatter.[28]

Toward the close of the fourth century B. C.,
the Greek city-states weakened, declined, and
came under the domination of the Macedonians,
Philip and Alexander. The latter's conquests
carried Greek learning and Greek economic customs to the East and brought back knowledge
of the Eastern world and its wares. Altho a conquering military imperialist, Alexander was
fully alive to the importance of organizing centers of trade in any process of building an empire, and he founded some seventy new cities
to be centers of commerce. He was indeed aware
that the resources of a military empire can be
obtained not only from careful husbandry but
by promoting industry and trade. However, in
spite of his strictly commercial efforts and in

spite of the introduction of coinage in the lands
east of the Mediterranean by means of his conquering and exploring expeditions, significant
progress in the evolution of business economy
was delayed until the establishment of the
Roman Empire.

The nominal date for the foundation of Rome
is 753 B. C., when the Latin town of Alba Longa
seems to have been established on the south
bank of the river Tiber, about fifteen miles from
the sea. A union was made with the people of a
Sabine town called Quirium or Curium which
had been established on a neighboring hill, and
with the Etruscans who had located on the north
side of the Tiber. The result was Rome. The government of this union was probably a monarchy
until about 500 B. C., when began a long series of
struggles between the Patricians and the Ple-
beians. This internal dissension continued until
the passage of the Licinian laws in 366 B. C.,
and the Publilian laws in 339 B. C., measures
which established the Roman constitution as a
moderate democracy. The energies of Rome were
freed for conquest, and the way was opened for
the Republic to become something more than
a city-state. Under the aggressive leadership of
her Senate of three hundred, Rome ruled all of
Italy by 275 B. C., and had annexed most of the
Mediterranean basin by 150 B. C. Then came revolts, assassinations, and massacres—revolts of

the Italians, revolts of the provincials—which persisted until the exhausted combatants welcomed the strong rule of one man, Augustus Cæsar, and the transition from Republic to Empire (31 B. C.-14 A. D.). Under the Empire, conquests continued until 117 A. D., when the limit seems to have been reached. In the third century A. D. the Empire began to break up, and the city itself fell before Alaric in 410 A. D. and before the Vandals again in 455 A. D.

The Romans, like the Greeks, were not primarily an industrial or a commercial people. They were "warriors and pillagers" during the period of the Republic and "administrators and builders" during the period of the Empire. They were never artisans and traders in any important degree. Their great contribution was *pax Romana,* Roman peace, which continued throughout the Empire and which meant respect for property and the rights of contract as well as an opportunity for commercial development and an enlarged knowledge of the goods of the world.

In their early history, the Romans devoted themselves to agriculture and learned the artisan trades from the Etruscans. With the growth of the Empire, agriculture was neglected and Rome became dependent upon outside regions for her food supply. Manufactured goods, too, were imported into Rome—not sent in quantity thence to other lands. There were plenty of artisan-producers on a small scale, but they merely supplied the home demand. Goldsmiths, shoemakers, sandal-makers, weavers, and dyers carried on a considerable business, but their products were needed by the inhabitants of Italy —even by the people of the Roman city. Necessities and luxuries came to Rome as imports to be paid for by money-tribute exacted from the provinces. In the early days, cattle and other forms of goods served as money. Two hundred or more years after the founding of Rome, fines were imposed in cattle and sheep. Still later, provision was made for commuting fines in current money termed *asses,* bronze or copper coins. About 269 B. C., Rome first issued the silver *denarius,* which became legal tender everywhere. By the first century B. C. gold coinage became more common, tho coins of small denomination were still struck from silver and copper.[29]

The Roman citizen was an adept bookkeeper and made careful entries of all his transactions. He kept his accounts in a book called "The Book of the Received and the Book of the Paid Away," using two columns for the record, corresponding roughly to the debit and credit placement of the present day. Roman weights and measures were standardized and were used for all official dealings. The provinces were allowed certain privileges in the use of local weights and measures, but these were always placed at a fixed ratio to the Roman standard.

Banking combined money-changing and money-lending. Rome was a gathering-place for people from all parts of the then-known world, and the presence of different forms of money provided the money-changers with plenty of activity in reducing the varied coins to a common standard. These banking negotiators accepted deposits, managed checking accounts, sold drafts and bills of exchange on distant cities, dealt in securities, carried accounts for the politicians, and lent money to farmers, merchants, and manufacturers.[30] Interest rates became so excessive that the government interfered, and in 51 B. C. twelve per cent. was made the legal rate by the Senate, altho much higher rates than twelve per cent. continued to prevail in the provinces. In the third and second centuries the publicans were the most prominent of capitalists, since they dealt with the State. They collected the tribute of the provinces on a contract basis and found opportunities for such extortionate profits that the word "publican" was hated by the populace and became a by-word among the Jews. They gathered the revenue from public pastures and farmed the customs. As contractors they worked the mines of Spain and the quarries of every province. They built the highways, harbors, and basilicas.

As the Roman State had no administrative
agencies for executing such projects directly, it
let them at auction to companies of promoters
headed by the Morgans, Vanderbilts, and Goulds
of that period—masterful capitalists whose aug-
menting riches and luxurious lives shocked stern
old patricians drawing meager revenues from
estates tilled by slaves.[31]

Rome was the monetary center of the world
in the first century B. C. The associations of capitalists were carefully organized as partnerships
or joint-stock companies managed on behalf of
the shareholders by *participes*. The Forum, with
its *basilicæ*, was crowded with *publicani* and
negotiatores haggling and closing speculative
transactions in an immense stock exchange. Under the Empire the opportunities for speculators and contractors were gradually reduced
and their operations were more systematically
supervised. The capitalists were mercilessly
squeezed as rascals whom it "was fair to pillage when opportunity arose." The frightful de-
basement of the currency, by which emperor
after emperor attempted to obtain the means
of paying his troops, paralyzed business so that
accumulated wealth was hoarded rather than
invested and private enterprise declined. It became necessary for the State to make increased
efforts to organize industrial and commercial
undertakings. The pressure of an expensive, excessive, and inefficient administration broke the

back of the money economy. Indeed, it can be safely said that "the ruin of the provinces in republican times had been due to the operations of private capitalists; in the Roman Empire it was at least accelerated and accentuated by the pressure of public burdens." [32]

Roman merchants were classed as wholesalers and retailers. The latter were mostly freed slaves, aliens, and members of the lowest classes. They were looked upon with contempt, debarred from the legions, and assigned to the protection of the god of thieves. Cicero expressed the common Roman prejudice when he said that the same people should not be the commanders of the world and the carriers of the world, and that retail trade was sordid and could thrive only by lying. In the early days of Rome the Forum was the principal market-place, but it eventually became a monetary and speculative exchange. One by one the markets were excluded from the Forum. The objectionable ones left first, the fish market, then the cattle market, and so on. In the later Empire fine shops were to be found on the Campus Martius, and markets grouped themselves in definite places to such an extent that streets were named for particular trades, the grain merchants' street, the belt-makers' street, the sandal-makers' street, and others. Some merchants, it is certain, made very definite use of signboard advertising, using sym-

bols to designate particular kinds of shops, such
as the sign of the bush for the wine shop, the
painted cow for the dairyman, and the mule
turning a mill for the bakery. Here, too, we find
the beginnings of copy-writing painted on walls
in black and red. One such advertisement ran
as follows:

IN THE ARRIAN
POLLIAN BLOCK OF HOUSES
THE PROPERTY OF CN ALIFUS NIGIDIUS
SENIOR
ARE TO BE LET FROM THE FIRST IDES OF
JULY
SHOPS WITH THEIR BOWERS
AND GENTLEMEN'S APARTMENTS
THE HIRER MUST APPLY TO THE SLAVE
OF CN ALIFUS NIGIDIUS SENIOR [23]

With the decline of the Roman rule, the pecuniary substructure began to go to pieces. The
Gothic hordes poured out of the wilds of northern and northeastern Europe. The "Roman
Peace" was ended and darkness closed down
upon the Western world. Pillage became more
profitable than commerce or industry; "petty
warfare became a chronic misery; the admirable
Roman roads fell into disrepair; commerce
shrank to a dribble of luxuries for the powerful and a local exchange of indispensables like
iron, salt, and tar for the commonalty; manufacturing for a wide market almost disappeared;
coinage became scanty, irregular and incredibly

confused." [34] Rome had run its tether. By 476
A. D., even the shadow of authority had passed
from the Roman Emperor of the West to the
eastern capital, Constantinople. Business economy reverted to furtive bartering and the European world passed into the "Dark Ages."

III

THE MEDIEVAL EXPERIMENTS

THE STORY of economy in the "Middle Ages"
covers a period of about one thousand years,
extending from the close of the fifth to the end
of the fifteenth century of the Christian Era.
The early centuries in this span are often called
the "Dark Ages" because they were almost barren of any achievements making for the permanent progress of mankind. When, in the fifth
century, the Roman Empire vanished from the
West and the barbarians entered into possession,
for a time, progress ceased. Society became rough
and turbulent. With each successive wave of
barbarian invasion, confusion and disorder deepened. Economic conditions returned to the primitive. Commerce was practically abandoned. The
light of the Ancient World of the West was ex-
tinguished.

Quite different, however, is the chronicle of
the Byzantine Empire of the East. Byzantium,
refounded as Constantinople and made the capital of the East by Constantine (326-333 A. D.),
presented a bulwark which successfully resisted
the shocks that shattered the civilization of the
West. For more than a thousand years, this
hardy city held its own as the protector of

Romano-Hellenic civilization. As each century came, a new horde of invaders besieged. In the fourth century, immediately after its establishment, Constantinople was threatened by the Goths; in the fifth, by Huns and Vandals; in the sixth, by Slavs; in the seventh, by Arabs and Persians; in the eighth and ninth, by Magyars, Bulgars and Russians. Not till 1453, however, did it utterly succumb.[1]

Here the money-economy suffered no such eclipse as in western Europe. "Gold coinage, a banking system, manufacturing on a considerable scale, a commerce which tapped the Orient on one side and the western Mediterranean on the other side, were maintained and in some respects elaborated."[2] Justinian (527-565 A. D.), probably the greatest of the emperors of the Eastern Empire, was fully alive to the importance of business. Care for commerce and trade is one of the most important features of his reign. His conquests reestablished communication and commerce with the western Mediterranean, and he was active in promoting trade both in the East and the West. He established *commerciarii*, trade depots, for the collection of customs and the purchase of raw silk from the barbarians.[3] Indeed, he introduced on a large scale the practise of selling monopolies or exclusive rights to engage in some special form of business enterprise, and used these revenues to restore and to construct magnificent public buildings. His monuments, churches, and parks astounded visitors from the West and testified to the skill of his architects and the lavishness of his taste.

The contribution of the Byzantine Empire is highly important because it is a contribution of conservation without which the reestablishment of business economy in western and northern Europe would have been immeasurably retarded and delayed. Constantinople preserved the essential structure of business economy, so that, "as order was gradually restored in Spain and Italy, in France and England, the new peoples might recover what their forefathers had destroyed when they devastated the Roman provinces." [4]

What the Byzantines conserved, the Saracens passed on to the new peoples of the West. When Europe groped in the darkness, the light of learning and of business came through the Saracens. These roving conquerors were those Arabs who accepted Islam, the followers of Mohammed (born about 570 A. D.). This "dreamer of the desert" began his prophetic séances and religious teaching when he was about forty years of age. Slowly but surely he aroused the semi-nomadic tribes of Arabia, and stimulated in them a religious zeal to "win the joys of Paradise by the subjugation and conversion of the earth.'' Very soon the new religion began to take on the ruthless and sordid features of conquest and tribute. In 629, Mohammed captured the holy city, Mecca, completed the conquest of Arabia, and, after calling on the King of Persia and the Byzantine Emperor to embrace Islamism, prepared to march beyond the borders of Arabia. At this juncture he died, cut off by a fever at Medina in 632 A. D.

The leaders who came after Mohammed, called his Caliphs or Successors, continued his campaign of conquest. Their success was rapid. By 639 all Syria and Egypt had been conquered. Persia soon fell an easy prey. In Africa, however, the Moslems met a long and stout resistance. Carthage did not fall until 697-698 and the North African conquest was not complete until 709. In 711-713, the Saracens crossed over into Spain from Mauritania, the modern Morocco, and overthrew the Visigoths. As early as 669, the Moslems attacked Constantinople but were repulsed. Their efforts to enter Europe by the east continued for many years afterward, but success did not come to them in or beyond the west of Asia Minor. The stronghold of Saracen power was in Egypt, Spain, and about the north of the Arabian desert. In Spain, the Moslem rule came to its height about the middle of the tenth century. The Moors, natives of North Africa, were summoned by the Saracens to aid against the advancing power of the Christians. About 1036 the Moors, in turn, overthrew the caliphate of Cordoba and the real Moorish dominion in southern Spain began. The Saracens did not adapt themselves to the people among whom they lived. Their religion made them exclusive, and when the fanaticism of their religious conquest had passed, their power declined. In the East, there came a gradual breaking-up of Saracen power, a separation into the earlier tribal organizations. In Spain, the Moors were driven to the south in 1238 and were conquered in 1491.

It was no race of rude and savage vandals that secured such a foothold in the southern part of the Continent. The Arabs liked and practised commerce long before the rise of Mohammed. The armies prepared the way for caravans in Asia and Africa, and Moslem merchants traveled by roads in every direction. Arabian sailors voyaged over the Red Sea and the Sea of Oman, penetrating as far as Hindustan and Indo-China. Ships from Alexandria and Syria thronged the harbors of Almeria and other Spanish ports. The harbors of Tripoli, Tunis, and Tangiers inherited the fortunes of vandal Carthage. Egypt, wisely governed, preserved her old fertility. Bagdad rivaled Constantinople as the market and metropolis of the world. There the Caliphs lived in all the luxury of the

THE MEDIEVAL EXPERIMENTS

Arabian Nights. Palaces ornamented with marble columns and rich carpets manufactured in the East, superb gardens refreshed by marble fountains falling into marble basins, a profusion of silken materials from India, an abundance of precious stones, every refinement of luxury and magnificence—this scarcely describes the pomp of the Caliphs, who lavished thus the tributes levied from a hundred races.

We hear of the Market of the Perfumers, the Market of the Money-Changers, the Straw Merchants' Bridge, the Fief of the Carpet-Spreaders, the Hay Market, the Gate of the Horse Market, the Tanners' Yard, the Four Markets, the Upper Barley Gate, the Silk House, the Slaves' Barracks, the Road of the Cages, the Fullers' Road, the Gatehouse of the Date Market, the Needle-Makers' Wharf, the Archway of the Armorers, the Cotton Market. In one part of the city Chinese goods were for sale, in another the famous Attabi stuffs (whence our expression "tabby cat"), woven in variegated colors of a mixture of silk and cotton. Here paper was manufactured of rags at a time when the West had lost the papyrus of antiquity and was forced to write all its manuscripts upon parchment made of sheepskin. Paper was originally discovered by the Chinese and was introduced among the Arabs in the eighth century, when factories were established at Samarkand and Bagdad. In Bagdad, too, was a mill with a hundred millstones, said to have been built for an early Caliph by a Byzantine ambassador possessed of engineering skill. There were lanes lined with great warehouses and streets crowded with shops and bazaars—twenty-four shops of the weavers of palm baskets, forty-three shops of perfume distillers, sixteen shops of drawers of golden wire, and over a hundred booksellers' establishments.[6]

In scarcely less degree, the Saracens carried their enterprise to Spain. They introduced rice, cotton, the sugar-cane, and the date-palm into Spain. Their ingenuity counteracted the dryness of the climate by skilful irrigation, and aqueducts conveyed the water preserved in artificial ponds. They filled the Spanish towns with manufactures of silk, cotton, and cloth. They taught the use of indigo and cochineal; they instructed in the art of fashioning porcelain-colored earthenware. They made linen paper and spread the knowledge of making paper from cotton and silk. The leathers of Cordoba and the well-tempered weapons of Toledo were famous. Spain maintained a large commerce, and the Caliphs of Cordoba had at least a thousand ships in their fleets. In fact, the whole economic character of Spain was changed and developed by the Saracen conquest, and Spain began to act as an intermediary for the instruction of other regions. The Saracen invasion was one of the means by which the East and the influence of its business economy came to the darkened West.

In the Teutonic world of the Franks—France and Germany—there is little record of significant commercial activity or business economy until the reign of Karl the Great, or Charlemagne (768-814). As was the case with all the rulers of the age, this early German soldier-king devoted much of his time and energy to war and conquest. In 773 he marched into Italy at the request of the pope, made war upon the advancing Lombards, deposed their king, and had himself crowned king of the Lombards in 774. In Spain, he took from the Saracens the territory as far as the Ebro (778). He proceeded to Rome. On Christmas Day, 800 A.D., as Charlemagne knelt on the steps of the altar at divine service in the basilica of St. Peter, Pope Leo III placed upon his brow the diadem of the Cæsars, and saluted him as "Emperor of the West" by the title of Charles I, Cæsar Augustus. His conquests continued as he fought bitterly against the Bavarians, the Saxons, the Avars, the Danes, and the Slavs. His empire finally extended over what is now the northeast of Spain, the whole of France and of northern and central Germany (except eastern Prussia), much of Austria, and all northern and central Italy, with the island of Corsica.

Charlemagne, however, was more than a conqueror. He first consolidated Christianity into a political form proceeding from itself, and he established the principle of hereditary monarchy. He actively promoted agriculture, manufactures, and commerce. Routes of trade were reestablished and fleets were stationed at strategic points as a protection for commerce. The Roman roads, bridges and aqueducts were put into repair. A great canal was built between the Rhine and the Danube. Charlemagne improved agriculture by requiring his subjects to plant various kinds of fruit trees. His capitulary, *De villis,* goes into minute details of farm life such as the care of bees and poultry, the dairy, and the making of wine.[6] He encouraged the accurate keeping of accounts and a general taking of stock at the beginning of every new year. He cultivated friendly relations with distant rulers for purposes of trade and in 796 A.D. signed what is certainly one of the earliest commercial treaties, the treaty with Offa, king of Mercia. In this document, Charles I promised protection to English traders coming from Mercia. "We also will," says Charlemagne, "that merchants shall have lawful protection in our kingdom according to our command; and if they be in any place unjustly aggrieved, let them apply to us or our judges, and we shall take care that ample justice be done them."[7] Steps were taken, too, toward the reformation of the standards of weights and measures. The emperor restored to the crown the exclusive right of coining money, and made an effort to establish a general system of currency based upon the pound of silver as a unit, the unit of currency thus corresponding to the unit of weight. This pound, or *libra,* gave its name to the English £ sterling and the French *livre,* and contained originally the equivalent of a pound weight of silver. In fact, Charlemagne's system of coinage was introduced in all western European countries, including England and Scotland.

Charles founded an empire which his successors could not rule, and following his death (814) its dissolution was rapid. But tho it fell, its effects remained. Charlemagne created Germany and bequeathed to its ruler the title of Roman emperor, thus uniting the Roman and the Teuton, "the memories and the civilization of the South and the fresh energy of the North." He disciplined the new populations of his empire and forced them to adopt agricultural life; and throughout central Europe he planted bishoprics and abbeys that became the distributing centers of knowledge. His powerful hands kneaded together the materials of modern Europe. His empire was dismembered by the treaty of Verdun (843), but the pieces formed nations. The treaty recognized an East Frankish and a West Frankish kingdom. The former became Germany; the latter, France. Italy, too, was recognized, and here we have the beginnings of modern nations.

As the Frankish empire disintegrated, central government and common action ceased to exist. The repeated incursions of Northmen, Magyars, and Saracens broke down communications and left each locality in isolation to look after itself. Other than political bonds had to be found to hold society together and to insure each individual some sort of order and protection. These bonds were discovered in personal relations between men and in dependent land tenure, in that strange collection of rules and practises which is commonly called feudalism. The word *feudum*, from which "feudalism" is derived, is not found in written documents until the time of Charles the Fat (884-887), but the system was firmly established long before. In fact, broadly speaking, feudalism is not peculiar to medieval Europe "but is found, in its essential features, wherever powers of government are exercised by landowners in virtue of their occupation of land."[8] Ancient Egypt and modern Japan have experienced similar developments. Nevertheless, the historic feudalism is that which grew up after the barbarian invasions, and which began to flourish in the ninth and tenth centuries.

The system itself is a kind of combination of

the old Roman method of granting land (by the State and not by a lord) to men in return for military service, and of the Teutonic custom of men following a chief as their personal lord, and standing in close personal relation to him. The transformation of the fragmentary elements of feudalism into a complicated institution was slow and gradual. The process was somewhat as follows:

> Gradually, in all parts of the West, kings came to recognize their impotence to dispense justice and organize the public security. Extensive grants of immunity from the jurisdiction of the royal officers tended to sever the connection between the king's palace and the outlying districts. A further step towards feudalism was taken when kings began to acquiesce in the principle that the landowner, as such, had a right to establish a court and exercise governmental rights over his tenants. The landowner, on his part, ceased to be content with the *benefice* which gave him no more than a life interest, without power of alienation. The king was compelled to recognize the principle of hereditary succession. Finally, the discovery that heavily armed cavalry was indispensable for success in warfare led to the endowment of *knights* with sufficient land to furnish the means for their equipment.

> Feudalism thus came into existence as a military measure to organize local defense; economically, to safeguard cultivation of the soil; and politically, to provide machinery for local administration of justice.[9]

OUTLINE OF BUSINESS

The central institution of feudalism is the *fief,* which is usually, but not in every case, land. The lord might grant to his vassal a certain lucrative office, or some definite ecclesiastical revenue, for which the recipient would engage to perform certain services. Normally, the fief was an estate of land large enough to support at least one armed knight and his war horse. At first these grants were for life only, then for two or three lives, and finally they became hereditary. A new heir was called upon to pay a sum equivalent to one year's revenue of the estate, as a *relief* on succession to the fief. The *relief* was a token of the lord's ultimate ownership of the land. The fief could not be *alienated,* willed, given, or sold to an outsider in the event of the absence of an heir. It reverted or *escheated* to the granting lord. The recipient of a fief entered into a personal bond with the granting lord, promising homage, fealty, and general or specific service. These services included military and agricultural services in the main, but at times included lighting the lord's way to bed with a candle, "counting his chessmen on Christmas Day," or even supporting his noble head during a rough passage on the Sea or the Channel. The *serfs* were the peasants who were sold or transferred with the land upon which they labored. They were slaves to the soil and inherited their status. A serf succeeded to the land of his father. Besides attempting to raise a scanty crop on his own land for his own sustenance, the serf was required to work the land of his lord, sometimes as many as four days a week. Even of his own wheat and oats and barley, the serf was obliged to hand over a part to his lord. The *villa* was the name for a large estate. In England the Norman word *manor* came to be used in the same meaning. The manor was self-sufficient: it constituted a small world by itself. It contained a manor house, residences for those who worked on the lands outside, a few homes for such artizans as smiths and carpenters, a mill, and a church. It was an economic, judicial, and religious unit.

Under feudalism, the State split up into tiny pieces. Europe was covered with a network of fiefs. In France alone, during the tenth century, the number of little governments of this kind is supposed to have exceeded 10,000.[10] Certainly, feudalism existed in its most highly developed form in the north and east of France, where by the fourteenth century the rule "no land without a lord" was somewhat sharply applied. In southern France, many landowners recognized no feudal overlords. In Normandy, serfdom disappeared early. In England, feudalism was prevalent before the Norman Conquest and was introduced in a more developed form by William the Conqueror.

The progress of business or money economy under such a system was definitely retarded and almost halted. The ideal of the manor was self-sufficiency; estate management for subsistence, not for revenue.

> With regard to the main product, food staples, the result was an alternation of *waste* and *want*. A good year brought a surplus for which there was no market outside the village, and which could not be worked up inside for lack of manufacturing skill and implements. A bad harvest, on the other hand, meant serious suffering, because there was no opportunity to buy food supplies outside the manor and bring them to it. Nearly every year was marked by a famine in one part or another of a country, and famine was often followed by pestilence.[11]

The rapid decay of Charlemagne's empire had destroyed the uniformity of his system of coinage. Many debasements of currency occurred. Local issues were coined by feudal lords in hundreds of places. In England, for example, under the disorderly reign of Stephen, nearly every baron had a mint in his castle.[12] Depreciations became perfectly reckless. Trading was mostly by barter until the fourteenth century. At every point, feudalism cramped and confined the development of a business economy. Payment in services, goods, or fiefs was an essential part of the feudal relation.

Strangely enough, the first glimmer of a developing business economy came to the western world in the series of religious expeditions known as the Crusades during the eleventh, twelfth, and thirteenth centuries. The word crusade means "war of the cross," from the French *croisade* (Provençal *crozada,* from *croz;* Latin *crux,* a cross). These spectacular expeditions had as their objects the recovery of the Holy Land —Palestine—from the Saracens and the Turks. From the fourth century on, religious pilgrimages to Jerusalem had been common, and for a long time the fact that the sepulcher of Christ, in particular, was in the possession of infidels had been felt as a reproach to Christendom. When the Turks succeeded the Saracens in power in Jerusalem, both the native Christians and the pilgrims were persecuted. Stories of these persecutions were carried to and exaggerated in the West. At the end of the year 1095 Pope Urban II summoned a great council at Clermont, in the south of France, a council which was attended by cardinals, prelates, and a great group of feudal lords. The Pope addressed the assembly in a stirring speech which found an instant response. When from the thousands of hearers the cry arose, "God wills it!" the speaker exhorted: "It is indeed the will of God, and let this memorable word be forever adopted as your cry of battle to animate the devotion and courage of the champions of Christ.

His cross is the symbol of your salvation; wear it, a red, a bloody cross, as an external mark on your breast or shoulders, as a pledge of your sacred and irrevocable engagement." So, in 1096, the followers of the bloody cross, probably a hundred thousand strong, launched their first attack on the Moslem.

There were eight principal and many minor crusades from 1096 to 1270. The early crusaders went overland across Europe because of the inadequacy of shipping in 1096. Later crusades followed the sea route, and the Italians profited handsomely as contractors for transportation and supplies. In fact, the fourth crusade (about 1200) was used by the Venetians to capture Constantinople. Probably the improvident feudal knights could not pay the Venetian transportation charges, so Venice forced them as debtors to aid her in extending her commercial territory. In the various crusades it has been estimated that a million men took part. The expeditions appealed to the devout, the adventurous, the romantic, the mercenary, and the curious. Moreover, the crusades offered an escape from feudal servitude, for the Church induced enlistments by interfering with feudal contracts, freeing men from the payment of interest and from the power of their feudal lords.[13] In the later crusades, such material privileges as permission to mortgage lands without the consent of the lords, and protection and subsistence for families left behind, were offered to induce men to take the cross.[14]

The effect of the crusades upon feudalism and upon the revival of business-like industry and commerce was tremendous. Coined money came to be increasingly used. Goods were far too bulky to carry on pilgrimages, and so those who followed the cross undertook to convert their wealth into money. Once more a money-economy began to succeed a system of barter. Gradually the change from the payment of feudal dues in services to payment in money-taxes was made. New wants and the taste for luxuries came to the West. The demand increased for the silks of China, the calicoes of India, the fine linen of Egypt, the gems of Africa. The spices of Arabia and India were sought to make more palatable the heavy and predominant meat diets of the feudal manor house. Carpets, furniture, window glass, and artificial light came into western use as new articles of consumption. Manufactures began to spring up. Windmills, brought from the East, stimulated industrial enterprise.

Moreover, there was a beginning in the increase of central authority over the feudal lords. Many lords went on the crusades never to return, while the kings stayed at home. Vacancies in many feudal holdings reverted to the princes from whom they had been secured.[15] Towns in

England, France, Germany, and the Low Countries bought their independence from feudal lords who wished money for crusading expeditions. As these free towns grew they became centers of hostility to feudalism. The extension of trade created wealth in money as well as in land. Feudalism was doomed; was, in short, slowly done to death by the growth of business economy.

The rise of the towns brought to the Middle Ages a new era in manufactures and general business progress. Altho their origins are in most cases lost in the past, the record indicates that after 1000 A. D., real towns grew up in constantly increasing numbers. Early medieval towns, of course, were imperfectly differentiated from the surrounding countryside. Gradually, however, the existence of fortifications, or of market facilities, determined their position. People found protection by nestling under the walls of some castle or monastery. Indeed, it is thought that the invasions of the Northmen and Hungarians caused the building of protecting walls about settlements and so contributed to the growth of towns.[16] The chance for profitable trade was sought, too, by the process of establishing the town at some break in a line of transportation, ''where goods had to be transshipped and where merchants would naturally congregate to rest and exchange their wares (cf.

Ox-ford, Cam-bridge, etc.)." [17] In the declining days of the Roman Empire and in the dark years of the early Middle Ages, men sought protection and the means of subsistence from others and thus bound themselves to feudal lords. From 1000 A. D. on, intensified by the effects of the crusades, men began to feel able to feed, clothe, and defend themselves. Then commenced their efforts to free themselves from their feudal lords. By the twelfth century, the more fortunate towns secured, by charter, certain liberties of buying and selling and claimed greater freedom. This greater independence was obtained by grant, purchase, or revolt.[18] The growth of these so-called free towns and cities was a distinct forward step in business and industrial progress. The towns were the "happy islands of peace" which "arose amidst the wide wasting ocean of violence and anarchy."

At first, unfortunately, the conscious business policy of the town was based on the ideal of self-sufficiency. Trade was held to be a local and municipal affair. Citizens of neighboring towns were treated as foreigners and subjected to heavy trading disabilities. Even within the town itself, business was highly restricted, for "only full burgesses were free to enjoy municipal privileges." [19] Late in the eleventh century, a further element of restriction grew up in the towns, the *gild*, merchant or craft.

The function of the gild was to maintain the monopoly of trading for its members. Outsiders, even if burgesses, were commonly prohibited from selling retail, and were subject to special toils. Entry into the gilds, tho sometimes on a hereditary basis, was normally through a stage of apprenticeship; and here again there were opportunities to exclude the many, and to confine the privileges of trading to a narrow oligarchy.[20]

The Anglo-Saxon word *gild* means a "contribution to a common fund" and came to be applied to almost any association or society of people engaged in a similar calling, or having a common purpose. Four kinds of gilds were prevalent: *religious gilds,* beneficial associations to aid the sick, and to furnish funeral benefits; *frith gilds,* mutual associations formed for the protection of members in legal affairs or in cases of violence and fraud; associations of traders known as *merchant gilds;* and associations of artisans termed *craft gilds.* Only the merchant and craft gilds need concern us here. As there grew up in the town a native merchant class of men who devoted most of their time to buying and selling, the need for organization appeared. Merchant gilds were formed to prevent or regulate outside competition and to serve the members of the association. These gilds extended their political power and were often practically identical with the municipal institutions of the town. They were granted the exclusive right of trading within the town. "Foreigners," people from any other town, were allowed to sell wares in the town at wholesale but could not sell at retail. The merchant gild sought to preserve a monopoly on trade for its own members.

The craft gilds were not less active. "They tried to secure good handiwork on the part of their members, and to suppress the production of goods by irresponsible people who were not members of the craft or 'mystery.' "[21] The regulations of the craft gilds divided laborers into apprentices, journeymen, and master-workmen, stipulated hours of labor, rates of wages, materials to be used in manufacture, and prices for products. Grants of monopoly were made to the craft gilds, and no one was allowed to practise a craft who did not belong to the appropriate gild.

Both forms of gilds had a good effect, at least at first, on the new development of business economy. While they were restrictive and monopolistic, they encouraged good workmanship and developed industrial and commercial groups within the towns. They became an essential institution of the town, and prepared the way for a more general organization representing the town as a whole. The grant of monopolistic privileges to a merchant or craft gild was commonly followed by concessions to all the townsmen.

Self-governing communities grew up as independent units in the midst of feudal society and feudal states.

The rise of towns reached its height at different periods in different parts of Europe. The Flemish towns led in the industrial development of western Europe. By 1200 there were some forty towns in Flanders, of which Bruges, Ghent, and Ypres had extensive industries. Manufactures of fine textiles, laces, carpets, leather goods, and metal work flourished and expanded. In Germany, the change from rural to town life did not become marked until the second half of the thirteenth century, when the free or imperial cities of Germany acquired their full powers of government in that confused period of anarchy following the death of Frederick II. By 1500 Hamburg had a hundred craft gilds, Cologne eighty, and Lübeck seventy. In the twelfth century, revolts against the nobles became increasingly common in France, and towns began to secure charters for government. Industry developed more slowly in France, but before the close of the medieval period, Paris and other cities were producing for export. Before 1100 towns in England were few and small. By the thirteenth century they began to grow as centers of influence and to multiply in number, but they did not reach the height of their medieval prosperity and independence until the fifteenth century. Nowhere in Europe, however, did the towns enjoy such complete independence and such widespread commercial activity as in Italy.

From 1000 to 1500 A. D., the Italians were the active trading people of Europe. In the declining days of Constantinople, energetic business men emigrated to Venice, Amalfi, Pisa, Genoa, and Florence, carrying with them their capital, as well as their skill in commerce and finance. A vigorous development of money-economy began.

Venice very largely bent her energies to the carrying trade. Altho her artizans produced glass, cloth, silk, leather, paper and soap in great quantities, the city was preeminently a city of great merchants rather than of small artizans. By the thirteenth century, Venetian traders were found throughout Europe. Conscious attempts were made to force all trade to flow through Venice. Foreign vessels were not permitted to cross directly between the east and west shores of the Adriatic, but were forced to go by way of Venice and unload at least two-thirds of their cargoes there. Venetian merchants were forbidden to ship their goods in foreign bottoms or to sell their vessels to foreigners. Visiting German merchants had to dispose of their entire stocks in Venice. The artizans of Venice were forbidden to practise their trades in foreign countries. The Rialto, or commercial exchange of Venice,

OUTLINE OF BUSINESS

became a tremendous business center. Private banks were numerous. The Bank of Venice, which is probably the oldest bank in Europe, was formulated in 1171 out of numerous bureaus which had been established to pay the interest on the first "permanent national debt." In 1280, Venice struck a gold coin called the ducat, which was of the same weight as the gold florin of Florence, struck in 1252. At the beginning of the fifteenth century it was reckoned that "there were at least a thousand nobles in the city whose income ranged from 4000 to 70,000 ducats each, and that at a time when 3000 ducats would buy a palace."

Florence gained her independence in the twelfth century and soon became the most famous inland Italian city. She built her greatness upon manufactures and financial operations. Her looms were the first to compete with success against the cloths of the East, and before the close of the medieval period, Florence had eighty-three factories for the production of silks and gold brocades.[22] She manufactured, as well, straw hats, artificial flowers, soaps, essences, perfumes, lacquered ware, glass, works in mosaics, metal, and alabaster, and even musical, mathematical, and scientific instruments. In order to sell her goods, make collections and exchanges, Florence established warehouses and banks at London, Bruges, Antwerp, Lyons, Avignon,

Geneva, Marseilles, and Provence. Merchants from all over Europe could draw on Florence for the settlement of their balances.

Forms of commercial paper (bills, checks, and notes), methods of keeping accounts, the transfer of credits—all were developed in the Italian cities.[23] In the thirteenth century, the Italians wrenched the trade in money from Jewish hands and Italian money-lenders established themselves in every land. The house of Peruzzi is reported to have had fourteen branches and one hundred and fifty agents in different parts of Europe. Nearly every great loan was effected through Italian agencies. North of the Alps almost any Italians engaged in banking were called "Lombards," and Lombard Street in London took its name from these Italian dealers in money. The name was applied as early as 1318.[24]

Simultaneously with the commercial activities of the Italian cities, the peoples of northern Europe were engaged in a similar enterprise on the coasts of the North Sea and the Baltic. The cities of Germany, in order to take advantage of the trade in the North, united in the Hansa or Hanseatic League, the most remarkable business association of the medieval period. A treaty between Lübeck and Hamburg in 1164 probably marks the beginning of the League, altho the name Hansa (an old Teutonic word meaning confederacy) was not applied to it until

1343, and it was not until 1368 that it became definitely organized. The aim of the League was to protect the commerce of the member cities from the attacks of pirates and feudal lords and to secure trading rights and privileges in countries abroad. The League varied greatly in membership and rose to the height of its power in the fourteenth and fifteenth centuries, when there were from sixty to eighty cities in the association. As the power of the various cities increased, the League became more ambitious. It endeavored to acquire a monopoly of the trade of the North. To gain this object, it obtained privileges and immunities from the northern kings by lending them money. Eventually, it secured almost a complete monopoly of the foreign trade of Denmark, Prussia, Russia, and Scandinavia. The League established "factories" or trading posts (not manufactories) at the central points of foreign trade, at Bergen, Bruges, London, Novgorod, and many other centers. Important privileges for these posts or factories were secured by treaties. Officials of the Hansa were recognized by the governing powers in all dealings between their own subjects and the Hansa merchants. Any merchant of any city in the League had the right to trade with any factory in the League and to enjoy its trading privileges. The factory was in the first place a fortress where Hansa merchants could be safe from attacks of the natives; in the second place, it was a place where trade could be regulated and where merchants could be held down to the strict rules of the Hanseatic Congress.

The government of the League was vested in a Congress of deputies which met once in three years or on special call. This Congress formulated decrees, passed them on to the member cities and to the "factories," and enforced the decrees with severity. A court was also held in the chief cities for the purpose of adjudicating matters pertaining to the League. The members of the League recognized the famous sea laws and ordinances of Wisby, an important Hansa town on the Island of Gothland. The principles of this law, in seventy chapters, have been embodied in all subsequent legislation governing maritime affairs and constitute the groundwork of modern marine jurisprudence.

The trade of the League was enormous. In exchange for the silks, velvets, fruits, sugar, and spices of the eastern countries, the Hansa merchants brought to the ports of England and the Netherlands fur and amber from the Baltic, and herrings, pitch, and timber from the countries of the North.

By 1500 it was apparent that the League had outlived its usefulness, and it began to disintegrate. Public order now prevailed, and commerce was reasonably safe. The local German princes threatened cities that did not withdraw from the League. The Dutch and the English began to make headway in trade. The opening of the new sea route to India by way of the Cape of Good Hope had its effect. The commerce of the East and West, which had been conducted in the ships of Pisa, Venice, and Genoa to the ports of London and Bruges, and thence by the Hanseatic traders to the ports of the Baltic, was now transferred to the countries on the Atlantic seaboard, whose ships had already become conspicuous in trade.

During the whole of the medieval period, the development of business economy in England was fitful and slow. On the side of trade, the Venetians and the Hanseatics fetched and carried for England. Even the ''Merchants of the Staple,'' who enjoyed a legal monopoly in the export of wool and sheepskins, leather, tin, and lead, were composed of aliens in the main. It was not until the very end of the Middle Ages that the native English merchants began to fight for privileges and rights equal to those extended to foreign merchants. On the side of money, progress was surer. Even in Anglo-Saxon times, the English kings began to commute the duties in kind upon exports and imports into money payments. Internal taxes and fines began to be collected in silver. A currency of silver pennies based on the Carolingian pound was struck. In

Stephen's time, to be sure, many bishops and barons coined money on their own account, but Henry II in 1180 called in all this base money. The first gold coins were struck in 1343 during the reign of Edward III. Besides debasing the currency from time to time, the English kings borrowed on a considerable scale from the Jews until their expulsion in 1290, and later from the Italian merchants and bankers.

At the close of the reign of Edward III, the lord of the manor had been reduced over a large part of England to the position of a modern landlord, receiving a rental in money from his tenants and becoming dependent for the cultivation of his own *demesne* on hired labor. The *villeinage* of early times had been gradually declining, and rent and wages were everywhere taking the place of *villein* tenure and forced service. The terrible ravages of the "Black Death," perhaps the most devastating plague of all history, halted economic progress in 1348, and resulted in the Statutes of Laborers of 1349, which attempted to drive the liberated serf back into his old position. The peasants revolted in 1381 under Wat Tyler, and while the revolt was suppressed, the death blow was dealt to serfdom.

Gradually, from the manors held by the Crown and by the Church, the commutation of week-work, boon-work and commodity payments into money rents spread to the lesser manors.

Gradually, too, the life of the people in the towns was reorganized on the basis of buying and selling. Crafts multiplied, merchants became more active, and a money economy was born. In 1404 Merchant Trading Companies began to be formed and by 1485 conditions were favorable for the opening of a new era in English business and commercial history.

By and large, medieval commerce was carried on under a "natural economy" (by barter) until the thirteenth century. From that time forward silver and gold money was increasingly used. But at no time were conditions such as to develop a complex business or money economy. Merchants could not rely upon governments to maintain standards of value. In many countries, coinage was debased again and again by ruling kings. Counterfeits were not rare, and the clipping of coin was common. Many of the great feudal lords stubbornly clung to their privileges of minting and issuing coins. The currency of medieval Europe was made up of a vast variety of coins which could not be passed at full value outside the localities where they were minted. The money-changer was a necessary figure, and after the thirteenth century was found even in the smallest towns, buying and selling the various coins in circulation. But while the money-changer facilitated payments in a particular town, he avoided the transportation of coin from

town to town and so was not very helpful to
the merchant who wished to make a payment in
some distant city. Until the rise of the Italian
banking houses of Bardi, Peruzzi, and the
Medici, the transmission of coinage was an ex-
ceedingly dangerous undertaking and the facili-
tation of commercial payments by letters of
credit and bills of exchange was infrequent indeed.

Commercial pursuits were not classified. Dealers of all kinds overlapped in functions. Pedlers
became shopkeepers and shopkeepers became
pedlers as commercial advantage beckoned.
Wholesale merchants supplied the retailers and
were generally prosperous, but even these traders did not specialize on particular wares or
confine their activities to wholesale trade. Markets were not continuous, but merely weekly or
semi-weekly. Trade was occasional, and even the
fairs were held semi-annually or annually more
often than quarterly. "The supply of goods was
not large enough, or regular enough, to make
trading permanent." [25]

It is perhaps safe to say that the medieval
fair is typical of commerce and trading during
the greater period of the Middle Ages. In the
first place, the measure of value accepted was
uncoined precious metal. In the second place, the
fair enjoyed a monopoly privilege. During the

usual six-weeks' term of a fair, all outside buying and selling was prohibited. "For the privileges given, the king and princes levied a toll on all goods brought to the fair, sold during its continuance, or taken away." The early fairs were held in connection with religious festivals. Later, side-shows in plenty, wild animals, actors, clowns, and gambling games grew up in the fairs to provide excitement for the boring and wearisome town and rural life. Partly social and partly commercial, fairs caught the fancy and spread all over the Continent and into England. Large and notable fairs were held at Bruges, Champagne, Paris, Leipzig, London, and Bristol.

Inside the fair, various special privileges were granted to merchants and particular trading institutions were developed. The most important of these was the Court of Pie Powder (Pie, French *pied*, foot; *curia pedis pulverizate*, court of the dusty foot) "from the dusty feet of the merchants, or, as some said, because justice was done as speedily as dust would fall from the foot." Here, cases of breach of contract, violations of the complicated rules for the rental of booths, and evasion of the weights and measures regulations were tried by a committee of traders. The court was highly prized because commercial law was in its infancy and because no justice for the merchant could be expected in a manorial or feudal court.

In fact, one of the wonders of the medieval period is that in spite of feudalism, localism, and the restrictions of town self-sufficiency, the business life of the Middle Ages evolved a "comprehensive but effective series" of associative and cooperative regulations and standards of trading and artizan behavior which were truly significant.

The formulation of such thirteenth and fourteenth century sea codes as that of the Hanseatic stronghold of Visby in the Baltic, of the Island of Oleron in the English Channel, and of the Catalan *consolat del mar* in the Mediterranean, maintained for centuries the basis of international shipping practise, integrity, and mutual confidence. Similarly the trade standards and usages of the gilds and of the great international fairs at Medina, Lyons, Leipzig, Frankfort, and elsewhere, which gradually crystallized into written ordinances, provided foundations for modern municipal institutions and for commercial and financial codes, many of which survive to this day. These were the symbols of that mutual trust which has always been the indispensable factor in all enduring business relations—the spirit which found expression in those early days in such usages as the phrase "easterling," or "sterling," as applied in confident acceptance at face value of the silver offered in trade at the London Steelyard by the "easterlings" from the Hanseatic towns around the Baltic and the North Sea.[20]

The Middle Ages were not "stagnant and unproductive." They bequeathed to the Modern World many economic inheritances "which could not have been obtained directly from classic antiquity." [27] Constantinople and the economic forces set in motion by the Saracens "acted as a leaven in the western world." The people progressed steadily from feudal oppression, and in the later centuries rapidly. By the fourteenth and fifteenth centuries, financial practise and organization elaborated. Developments in the manufacture of metals and textiles were notable. Merchant life was dignified and prosperous. New articles of consumption were widespread. Fresh desires and new ambitions ushered in a new period.

IV

THE MODERN ISSUE

THE FIVE HUNDRED YEARS which make up the so-called Modern Era are of supreme importance to the story of business economy. Within the comparatively brief limits of this short sweep of years, 1500-1929, are set greater changes in the economic substructure of civilization than are to be found in the records of any previous period. While the present is conditioned in no inconsiderable degree by the ancient and medieval, it has been influenced in a very special sense by the events of these last five hundred years.

For good or ill, by the latter part of the fifteenth century, mankind in western and central Europe had begun to think for itself, to test the reverential claims of long-established economic institutions, to reject much of the old, and to adopt much of the new. Instead of clinging to tradition as a guide through every maze, instead of keeping timidly in view the landmarks of the voyagers of the past, men everywhere set up "change" and "progress" as watchwords of their enduring conflict with the problems of economic existence. New beliefs, new values, and new institutions began to affect not only the business life of Europe (the Commercial Revolution) but also its intellectual life (the Renaissance) and its religious life (the Reformation). Emancipation from medieval trammels left men free to see many of the facts about them, to reason concerning these facts, and to act boldly upon resultant judgments. Thus, while gathering up the harvest of the past, they sowed the seed for new crops to ripen and flourish in the centuries to come.

In the later and brighter years of the Middle Ages, Europe began to shape itself into a system of organized territorial states. The driving force of trade prepared the way for the triumph of the national principle. From the towns and the city centers, commerce spread through the whole territories of the states, "weakening the great feudal landowners and powerfully assisting the monarchy, and its natural allies—the middle classes." For a long time, Europe had been roughly divided into those lands—like Portugal, Spain, and England—that produced raw material, and those—like Flanders and northern Italy—that made raw materials into finished goods and traded these products about the whole of the medieval world. But by the middle of the fifteenth century, the native merchants in these great raw-material-producing areas commenced to cast covetous eyes at the prosperity of established marts of trade. Portuguese, Spanish, and English merchants turned to their royal governments for help, for they had suffered much from the confusion of local laws and regulations, the multiplicity of tolls, and the diversity of coinage. They needed royal support to enter into a serious rivalry with Italy and Flanders. Very soon they became strong enough to represent their interests as national interests. Offensive and defensive alliances were struck between kings and merchants. "The king received the money wherewith to support a standing army, to enforce order on the king's highway, and hold the nobles to the king's peace; the merchants gained privileges and protection, and the effective help of royal fleets."

In divers ways these raw-material states prepared to win commercial leadership. Their sailors learned to leave the coast-lines and to steer boldly into the open ocean, secure in the consciousness that they were approaching not a "sea of darkness" but successive capes of "Good Hope" and at length the Indies. The exorbitant prices for spices demanded by the Italian merchants stimulated the search for new routes to the East.

The urge that drove the Portugese down the West Coast of Africa, leading to the accidental discovery of Brazil en route; the impulse that sped Columbus on that hazardous adventure across the dark wastes of the Atlantic, and the inspiration of the frantic efforts to break through the fogs of the Northwest Passage and of the

[105]

countless subsequent drives to penetrate the unknown wilderness of the new continent—nearly
all of these immortal episodes had as their chief
objectives the attainment of new trade routes to
the precious stores of spices in the East.

Pepper, cloves, and cinnamon were absolutely
indispensable for the heavily predominant meat
diets of Western Europe. . . . The only substitute for refrigeration was a profusion of spices;
and if there had been no such emphatic demand
for them issuing with increasing emphasis from
every kitchen in Western Europe as living standards improved, one wonders whether there would
have been any abiding persistence, any lasting
accomplishment, in all of the adventuring, all
of the fervid revival of the Crusader's spirit, all
of the hunting for the hated Moslem in the
Orient.[1]

The prosperity of the Western nations was
visibly bound up with the discovery and control
of new trade routes. The lure of the Indies ushered in the golden age of exploration and discovery which dawned during the late fifteenth
century and reached its zenith during the first
half of the sixteenth.

In this period of world-discoveries and grand
adventure, which brought about the Commercial
Revolution, the era of town or municipal commerce passed away forever. The Mediterranean
ceased to be the center of commercial and trading activity. Portugal, Spain, Holland, France,
and England succeeded to the greatness and

prosperity of Venice and Genoa. The expeditions which these nations sent forth to the lands of silk and spice succeeded beyond their dreams in turning the streams of commerce to their ports. Among these new masters of the seas, the peoples of the Atlantic seaboard, national consciousness was strongly developed, and centralized governments were at least partially perfected. The feeble governments of the medieval period were replaced by national monarchies. This national spirit was carried into commerce. Portugal (from 1420 to 1580) and Spain (from 1479 to 1588) owed their trade and commerce to the enterprise of their royal families. Holland gained a trade route as an incident of her struggle for national independence (from 1577 to 1648). England achieved commercial importance during the time of the Tudors (1485-1603). France was less active, but became a significant commercial power under the Bourbons.[2]

The development of business economy was rapid under the impetus of expanding trade. By the sixteenth century, "the uses of money had developed far enough in England to make the inflow of Mexican and Peruvian silver from Spain produce grave social results." An abundance of silver began to come from the West Indies in 1516 and from Mexico in 1522. The discovery, in 1557, of a simpler process of reducing the ore, by means of Spanish quicksilver, de-

creased the cost of production, and still further
augmented the yield of bullion.

> In 1553, the Spaniards had obtained access to
> Peru, from which additional supplies of silver
> could be obtained. Despite the efforts of the
> Spaniards to retain this treasure in their own
> hands, it soon began to circulate in Europe; and
> a share of it was brought to England, especially,
> as we may believe, for the purchase of wool
> and cloth.[3]

This influx of silver had its effect on general
prices (prices rose) and severely strained the
circumstances of the landed gentry by reducing
the value of the money payments into which
feudal dues had been commuted. However, the
new supplies of precious metals gave a powerful
impetus to commercial enterprise and made it
possible for the sixteenth-century merchant to
finance big undertakings. England, which had
been mainly a self-contained raw-material-producing state, entered upon a career of colonizing.

The era of colonization begins in the sixteenth century. The dazzling riches of Aztec and
Inca, the "curious incense burners of the West
Indies called tabacos," the possibilities of cheap
imports of sugar, coffee, cotton, rubber, cabinet
woods, etc., directed attention towards colonies
as a means of supplementing the economic resources of the mother country. The new nations
of Western Europe recognized the necessity of

founding their power not on "the fearlessness of their chevaliers," but on the extent of their financial resources.

> In endeavoring to cultivate and preserve the wealth of their subjects, European monarchs proceeded upon the assumption that if a nation exported costly manufactures to its own colonies and imported cheap raw materials from them, the money paid into the home country for manufactures would more than counterbalance the money paid out for raw materials, and this "favorable balance of trade" would bring gold to the nation.[4]

With this end in view, the European nations became vitally interested in the islands and the continents of the West, as well as in Africa, India, and the spice islands of the East.

As the scale of business undertakings grew, the one-man enterprise, and even the partnership, became inadequate to control the swelling trade. The most effective method of developing a lucrative colonial trade came to be by means of chartered commercial companies. The largest and most dangerous trading projects were carried on in the fifteenth and sixteenth centuries by "regulated companies." These companies were created by the Crown and were under royal regulation. They were composed of merchants, each of whom traded on his own account. The "Merchant Adventurers" Com-

pany was chartered to trade with the Low
Countries and Germany as early as 1505. In
1581 the Levant Company was regularly incorporated. England (in 1600), Holland (in 1602),
France (in 1664), Sweden, Denmark, Scotland,
and Prussia each chartered its own "East India
Company." The London and the Plymouth
Companies (1606) shared privileges in the English colonies on the Atlantic Coast of America.
The modern corporation had its birth in the
joint-stock companies which were the natural
outgrowth of the "regulated" companies.

After a decade or so, many of the regulated
companies found that individual members often
pursued their own special interests to the detri-
ment of the company's welfare. Consequently
they gradually required their members to con-
tribute to a common treasury, to entrust the
direction of the business to the most able members, and to receive their profits or dividends
in proportion to their shares in the general
treasury or "joint stock." The idea of a permanent whole company, but one in which each
individual could buy or sell "shares" in the
joint stock, caught the fancy, and most of the
chartered colonial companies organized on the
new basis. The joint-stock company began its
conquering career in England in the latter half
of the sixteenth century with the formation of
the Russia Company and the Adventurers to

Africa. The English East India Company, organized as a regulated company in 1600, was reorganized piecemeal for half a century until it, too, acquired the form of a joint-stock enterprise.[5]

With the growing complexity of business activities there was need for more accurate financial record-keeping. Before 1494, simple accounts were the rule, for it was an easy matter for stewards of estates to keep records of the work done and the commodities received from the tenantry and for the small merchants to depend upon memory and the most elementary pocket file. The mystery of double-entry bookkeeping— an Italian invention first published in 1494— led to more elaborate records and was widely adopted by the mercantile classes of England in the sixteenth century.[6]

Financial organization, too, became more elaborate. Antwerp presented in the sixteenth century the first instance of a great bourse or exchange, a place "in which men meet daily and effect their exchanges without displaying and transferring the wares themselves, by the use of paper securities representing the wares." The wares of the Antwerp exchange were paper instruments representing loanable capital. Here was collected loanable capital from all over Europe. Monarchs who formerly borrowed money from individual financiers like the South

German Fugger family now negotiated their loans on the Antwerp exchange.

Through the medium of the exchange a French king could and did borrow money of a Turkish pasha; and it is said that payments amounting to a million crowns were made in a single morning without the use of a penny of cash.[7]

Shares of public debt became the object of regular commerce and modern forms of speculation developed. Indeed, as early as 1542, there were complaints about speculating on the rise and fall of stocks, and the Antwerp exchange was called a "monstrous thing." By the beginning of the seventeenth century, the Antwerp exchange and the new exchange at Amsterdam began to attract capital not merely to be loaned on royal credit but to be invested in private or semi-private business undertakings. Shares of trading and industrial companies became active in exchange operations. Shares of the Dutch East India Company were put on the market in 1602 and shares of the English companies trading with Asia and Africa circulated freely on the Amsterdam exchange. The stock exchange was a natural accompaniment of the stock company.

In the early Middle Ages the practise of lending money for interest had been forbidden by the Christian Church. However, by the middle of the seventeenth century, the old doctrine of "usury" ceased to appeal to the conscience, and banking arose in England. The London goldsmiths possessed strong boxes because of their work with precious metals, and occasionally accepted the commissions of merchants and landowners for the safekeeping of money in these strong boxes. Very soon these enterprising goldsmiths discovered that they were never required to pay back more than a fraction of their total deposits in any given day or week and that consequently they could make profits by lending part of the moneys in their strong boxes. Soon they began to encourage deposits by paying interest to depositors. A tract of 1676 describes their operations as follows:

> Having thus got Money into their hands, they presumed upon some to come, as fast as others was paid away, and upon that confidence of a running Cash (as they call it) they begun to accomodate men with moneys for Weeks and Moneths, upon extraordinary gratuities, and supply all necessitous Merchants that overtraded their Stock, with present Money for their Bills of Exchange, discounting sometimes double, perhaps treble interest for the time, as they found the Merchant more or less pinched.[3]

They had become bankers of discount and deposit. Later they discovered that it was as easy to lend their promises to pay as it was to lend coin, and they became bankers of issue. Goldsmiths' notes were familiar currency among the wealthy. London developed into an important monetary center, and the goldsmith bankers exerted an important political influence in the time of the Stuarts (1603-1689), a considerable period before the Bank of England was established (1694).

The expansion of trade and the development of financial organization so that the sixteenth-century merchant was able to command accumulations of capital and to take advantage of the new machinery of credit was the strongest possible stimulus to manufacturing. In the Middle Ages, as has been noted, the prevailing organization of manufacturing was the gild system, under which the individual craftsman worked with his own tools on his own materials. The markets were largely local, their needs were well known and were subject to little fluctuation. With the development of widening markets, the accumulation of ample funds by business men, and the consequent opportunity for quantity production and standardization of products, a new organization of industry appeared.

This new system, the *domestic* system, established by the capitalists, marks the triumph of business enterprise over medieval craftsmanship. The domestic system of fabrication is distinguished from the gild system by the existence of a middleman or *entrepreneur* upon whom the domestic worker is dependent. Bankers, investors, and merchants, who possessed sufficient funds, furnished raw materials and tools, spinning wheels and looms to a large number of workers, fixed a rate of money payment for a given amount of work (irrespective of the market price of the finished article), and then received back and sold the finished products. The system was "domestic" because the work was done at home, and "capitalistic" because the raw materials and finished products were owned not by the workers who worked them but by a "capitalist." Such a system existed in the West of England woolen industry in the middle of the fifteenth century and at an earlier date in the tin-mining industry of Cornwall.[9] In Tudor England (1485-1603) the domestic system became widely used. Merchants and investors went outside the towns, "where gild restrictions were irksome, and built up new communities of small householders." By so doing, they escaped from the medievalism of the gild system, with all its rigid regulations and archaic restrictions. Business captured craftsmanship.

From 1558 to 1603, the "Great Lord Burleigh," first as Secretary of State for England and later as Lord Treasurer, made deliberate attempts to foster native industries and granted patents for new manufacturing enterprises.[10] English capitalists undertook new enterprises in glass manufacturing, starch manufacturing,

and sugar refining, as well as developing the
English woolen industry to new importance.
The political conditions of the time favored the
immigration of skilled artizans, and this influx
of skilled workers brought about a great expansion of new branches of cloth manufacture, and
the introduction—or improvement—of glass
manufacture, cutlery, paper-making, and other
trades.

With all the world-wide searchings for new
trade routes and the steady extension of trade
to the ends of the earth, commerce came home
to the mass of the English people. The occasional and periodical fairs of the Middle Ages
proved to be entirely inadequate to meet the
trading needs. As communities became less self-
sufficient, weekly markets sprang up, grew
quickly into daily markets, and persisted as
definitely established retail shops. Wholesale
supplies became more regular as facilities for
communication and transportation increased
and as a new class of merchants appeared, the
commission merchant or factor. Relays of horses
with postilions were established by governments,
and regular transportation routes aided greatly
in extending the volume and variety of trading.
In the sixteenth century a distance of seventy-
five miles (Strassburg to Basel) required eight
days' travel in a coach. In 1600 the same distance was covered by diligence in six days, and

in 1700 in four days. The commission merchants or factors specialized their business activities to such an extent that by the seventeenth century five classes of factors were distinguishable: "those who lived in a manufacturing or commercial center and bought goods for others; those who sold goods for others; the correspondents of business men and bankers who made collections and remittances of money for them; forwarders, who received and forwarded goods at places of transshipment; and, finally, the agents for carriers, who distributed and collected the load of a freight wagon in a city." [11] New wants, new desires for better things, and their increasing wholesale availability stimulated the retail trade so that by 1700 London and other English cities had a wide variety of retail shops doing business with large consuming clienteles. Symbolic shop-signs, shop-bills, trade-cards, various public registers of buying wants and selling offers, and even advertisements in the news-books, began to appear. In 1663, advertising in England had progressed to the point of royal notice. Roger L'Estrange was given a patent as "Surveyor of the Press," which included the exclusive privilege of "writing, printing, and publishing advertisements." Newspapers of the period of 1700, partially impelled by growing incomes from advertising, began to be issued twice and three times a week, and in 1702 the first English daily newspaper appeared—the London *Daily Courant*.

Agriculture, too, began to be bent beneath the sway of business economy. The sixteenth and seventeenth centuries witnessed, in many districts, significant departures from medieval techniques. Land management had been reconstituted on the basis of money economy in the fifteenth century and it now came to be regarded more generally from the point of view of possible profits. Tillage was pursued with a view to the markets, and the possibility of enhancing rents rendered it profitable to sink capital into improvement of the land. Wealthy investors had large sums of capital to invest. They put it into making agriculture more efficient and businesslike. "First in Holland and Flanders, then in England, a revolution in agriculture took place."

Attention was now concentrated on the discovery of improved rotation of crops, scientific animal husbandry, and more effective methods of cultivation. Those of the old farming population who could not pay the costs of enclosure (fencing and hedging), or adapt themselves to the business economy of making and living on money, either became wage-workers on the land or drifted into the towns. The capitalistic pioneers of the new methods were one and all advocates of enclosure.[12] It availed the small proprietors and cottagers not at all to cling to the idea of the homogeneous village with its open fields and common rights. Public opinion favored putting the land to its most profitable use and enclosures went on apace in the effort to increase the marketable food supplies.

> Throughout the seventeenth and eighteenth centuries, the enclosure of common waste and common fields was an outward and visible sign of the progress of improvement in the management of land. The primitive method of laying out the land of the freeholders and tenants as scattered strips in common fields, with pasture rights on the common waste, presented an obstacle to any changes for the better. The existence of common fields, cultivated by common custom, was a hindrance to improved husbandry; and the pasturage on common wastes was often spoiled from lack of better management.[13]

Between 1760 and 1797, some 1,500 Enclosure Acts were passed by the English Parliament consolidating strips and giving to every owner of strips and meadowland a share of land equal in value to what he had held, with the requirement of fencing and hedging the new holdings. In the latter part of the eighteenth century the common-fields system almost entirely disappeared. The advance in rents during the Napoleonic wars sent millions of small farmers into the towns and led to the consolidation of holdings.

The hold of business on English farming was complete.

These sixteenth-, seventeenth-, and early eighteenth-century changes in commerce and agriculture, usually called the Commercial and Agricultural Revolutions, were essential preliminaries to the so-called Industrial Revolution which was born in the north of England in the middle of the eighteenth century. Surplus capital became plentiful in 1715-1720, and a frenzy for speculation took possession of London. Promoters thrived, and "bubble" companies sprang up overnight. "Change alley became the vortex of a human whirlpool," as excited men and women of all ages and rank joined together in the "fierce pursuit of fortune." [14]

One company, with a capital of three million pounds, was "for insuring to all masters and mistresses the losses they may sustain by servants"; another was "for furnishing merchants and others with watches"; a third, with a capital of one million pounds, was "for a wheel for perpetual motion"; a fourth was for making salt water fresh; a fifth was launched by a clergyman for the extraordinary object of importing a number of large jackasses from Spain in order to improve the breed of mules in England—"as if," Mr. Fox Bourne grimly adds, "there were not already jackasses enough in London." This company proceeded so far that negotiations were actually opened for the purchase of immense tracts of marsh-lands for its purposes. [15]

The mania raged for months and culminated in the promotion of the South Sea Company. Finally, the government took a hand and commenced the prosecution of Blunt and his South Sea Company. At once the bubble companies collapsed and vanished like soap-bubbles at the prick of a pin.[16] The London brokers had learned their lesson and began to feel their way in the direction of the organization of a security exchange, which, however, did not materialize until 1773.

The significant truth which began to occupy men's minds in this period, 1720-1740, was that manufacturing was still on the very simple basis of the domestic system, while mercantile and banking affairs were organized on a large-scale basis. The enlargement of markets and the piling up of surplus capital that eagerly sought profitable investment began to provide a strong incentive for increased production. A dawning realization came to the capitalists that they could best secure and keep foreign markets, not by special privileges, but by producing goods at low costs, by making and selling goods that were better and cheaper than those of other countries. The need for new methods and new tools of production was felt. Enterprising business men had capital enough to be willing to run the risk of introducing new inventions in the hope of increasing production and lowering costs.

Under these circumstances it is not surprizing that a burst of inventive genius characterizes the eighteenth century. Inventions are seldom merely fortuitous; they are generally called forth by commercial need and favorable economic conditions for widespread trial.

The eighteenth-century revolution in methods of manufacture rightly begins in the textile trade. In 1738 Kay invented the flying shuttle for weaving cotton, a shuttle which made it possible for one man to manage a wide loom. From this point on, inventions in the textile field alternated between spinning and weaving machines. The Kay Shuttle made it easier to weave cloth than to spin thread. Greater supplies of thread were needed, and in response to the need Hargreaves produced the spinning-jenny in 1764, and Crompton the spinning-mule about 1774. Now the weavers could not keep up with the spinners until Edmund Cartwright's water-power loom was patented in 1787. The weavers and spinners were now "neck and neck," and able to make textiles on a large scale. The call for new supplies of raw material was soon answered by the invention of the cotton gin by the American Eli Whitney in 1793. Watt's steam engine, which was built on the work of other experimenters, was patented in 1769 and was first yoked to cotton-mill machinery in 1785.

The invention of the reverberatory furnace

in 1784 made possible the smelting of iron by the use of coal and alleviated England's shortage of charcoal. As a consequence, the iron industry had a rapid rise in the coal fields of the Midlands and North ("The Black Country"). Improvement in communication and transportation went hand-in-hand with increased production. From 1760 to 1774, the English Parliament passed 452 acts for road improvement. Telford (1756-1834) and McAdam (1756-1836) made a scientific study of the problems of road engineering. The superimposing of layers of broken and crushed stone with a smooth surface rounded to shed water persists as *macadam* road engineering to this day. By the year 1825, the average speed of coaches and diligences had been increased from six to nine miles per hour because of improved roads. Canals were built to connect the coalfields with the new manufacturing centers, and Brindley's Bridgewater Canal (1759) halved the price of coal in Manchester.[17] Railways began in the industrial North with the opening of the Stockton and Darlington line in 1825, which reduced the price of coal from 18 shillings to 8 shillings per ton. Robert Fulton put the Watt engine to work in the first commercially successful steamboat, the *Clermont*, on the Hudson River in 1807. The English General Steam Navigation Company was organized in 1824 in an effort to apply steam to sea traffic.

Ocean voyages began in 1837 and the sailing ship was doomed.

The immediate results of the whole process which is called the Industrial Revolution were increases in production, reductions in prices of fabricated articles, and decreases in town rents.[18] The proportion of men working on their own account grew smaller in all fields of enterprise, as did the number who consumed their own products, while the proportion of men working for wages increased.[19] Ultimately, the effect of the Industrial Revolution was to introduce large-scale factory production as the normal type of manufacturing in all industries. In the two brief generations, from 1770 to 1840, the whole aspect of England changed. It became an empire of factories, mills, and foundries. The great textile towns and the "Black Country" of the coal and iron industry grew up. The iron output rose from 17,000 tons in 1740 to 125,000 in 1796. Canals and railroads cut through the agricultural districts to connect the industries with each other and with the outside world. England was fairly launched on her career as a manufacturing nation under a full-fledged factory system.

In the early years of American colonization, "the stream of migration to America was almost purely English" and brought to our shores the ideas and usages of English business economy as it existed in the seventeenth century. The enormous task of wresting a living from primitive nature and the hardships entailed in protecting the little English hamlets from the harrowing raids of the Indian compelled the early settlers to adopt a simpler form of economy than that to which they were accustomed. Until 1750 coin was scarce and consisted mainly of specie from the Spanish and French West Indies and paper currency issued in the several colonies. Barter-trading and the use of commodity-currencies was common. Wampum, strings of shells, served for trading with the Indian. Codfish was used as a basis of reckoning values among the colonists in New England; bearskins were used in New York; wheat was the currency of Pennsylvania; tobacco the medium of exchange in Virginia. The sparse and scattered population made it necessary for the family to become self-sufficient after the fashion of medieval times. Household industries developed for the colonists were far too civilized to revert to the crude Indian mode of life. The self-sufficiency of the family group was the dominant feature of economic life until 1800. Specialization of occupation was impossible in the main. Complicated financial machinery was not needed and consequently did not come into existence. The chief aim of life was "to get enough food and clothing, to build houses and clear land, to keep off the Indians.''

While this simpler form of economy was short-lived on the Atlantic seaboard, it remained the characteristic economy of the pioneers who ''crept out into the narrow valleys, out into the deep forests, and high into the piedmont.'' [20] It passed westward with the frontier. By 1765 a huge agricultural area was already occupied and an immense stream of produce flowed to the port towns for shipment. Agriculture over-shadowed all other forms of enterprise. Crops were sure, so that advances from England in goods and in cash were easily obtained by colonial producers. Few of the colonists, however, ever caught up with these credit advances. Many colonists who were frightfully in arrears in 1770-1776 welcomed the Revolution because it offered a method of staying debt. During the Revolution and for the first thirty years of American independence, agriculture continued supreme, and manufacturing remained a house-hold matter. The United States lived on as an economic dependency of England.

With the hardships of the Long Embargo, and the War of 1812, thoughts began to turn to the development of native industries. The first pro-tective tariff law was passed in 1816 and men bent to the task of creating infant industries out of household crafts. Mills began to appear along the tumbling streams, and machinery took up some of the burden of labor.[21] By 1840, the factory system was firmly enough established to presage the industrialization of the whole country.

The industrial revolution began in earnest in 1860, nearly a century after its English beginning. The combination of great physical resources, a rapidly increasing population, and expanding railroad trackage created a large market which could be reached by large-scale manufacturers. The Civil War apparently stimulated the whole movement. The consolidation and unification of the Northern States for the purpose of repressing the rebellion set up the Northern Government as a huge purchasing market.

> The government itself became the largest purchaser of manufactured articles in the world, entering the market as a heavy buyer of munitions and supplies for its army and navy. The steady rise of the price level during and after the war period greatly increased the profitableness of business enterprise, while the far-sighted (or merely fortunate) men who borrowed money to build their establishments and were able, later on, to repay their debts in the depreciated national currency, thereby expedited the concentration of capital in industry.[22]

English inventions began to be "smuggled in and copied." American inventors added to the borrowed contrivances and evolved ingenious machines of their own, many of which facilitated the production and market-distribution of manufactured goods. In 1835 at New York University, Morse developed the telegraph, which shortly "spanned the continent, bringing around one table the business transactions of a whole nation." Davenport invented the electric motor in 1837, Fitch introduced the turret-lathe in 1845, Howe created the sewing-machine in 1846, Hoe developed the rotary press in 1847, Vail produced the electric locomotive in 1851, and Bessemer worked out the Bessemer steel process in 1865.

> For every inventor there stood a captain of industry ready to snatch the machine from the workshop, collect the capital to put it in motion, organize the labor forces necessary to production, and seek out the markets for the stream of goods that flowed from its whirling wheels.[33]

The latter half of the nineteenth century saw the accumulated momentum of industry and of a developing business economy "gathering speed with each swiftly passing decade." The production of pig iron jumped from 1.7 millions of tons in 1870 to 13.7 millions of tons in 1900; the production of steel from 0.07 to 10.2, the value of exports of iron, steel, and manufactures from 5 millions of dollars in 1860 to 121 millions of dollars in 1900. Grants, subsidies, and privileges were bestowed upon railroads, mining enterprises, and manufacturing concerns.[24] Between 1860 and 1900 the capital invested in manufacturing rose from one billion dollars to twelve billion dollars and the number of industrial wage earners from 1,500,000 to 5,500,000.[25] By 1890 America had nearly half the railway mileage of the world. Gradually but steadily the control of business enterprise shifted from the promoters or the operators of industry to the "directors of capital accumulations." Banks began to operate on a large scale and the New York Stock Exchange grew in importance as a financial trading center. The National Banking Act was passed in 1863, silver was demonetized in 1873, specie payments were resumed in 1879, and since that time no form of currency has been at a discount. The first significant foreign loan was floated by Morgan & Company in 1899. The financial organization of trading and of manufacturing became complex indeed.

At the end of the century three-fourths of the manufactured products came from factories owned by associations of stockholders; in each great industry was a network of federated plants under corporate direction; by 1890 combination was the supreme concept of the industrial magnate.[26]

In terms of material progress, a thousand years have elapsed since 1900, a century's span since 1914. The money value of manufactured products of the United States was about eleven billions of dollars in 1899 as opposed to sixty-one billions of dollars in 1923. In 1914 the combustion engine supplied only five per cent. of the horse-power in the United States. In 1928 it supplied more than the combined total of all other sources of power. The world's telephone-wire mileage was about 33.7 millions in 1913. By 1925 it had increased to 84.5 millions. Manufacturing efficiency grows on apace. Our steel production has increased 50 per cent. per worker since 1913. Each employee in the automobile industry is turning out 11.5 units (cars, trucks, etc.) as against 7.2 in 1913.[27] Truly we can say with Stuart Chase,

It was not until after the War that the sparks of mass production and automatic machinery, which we had been quietly nursing for some years, burst into flame, and stupefied the world. America did not invent mass production, indeed it is implicit in the technical evolution of the machine, but it developed the process beyond anything accomplished in other countries, and in the opinion of competent observers laid what amounted to a new industrial revolution upon the bed of the old.[28]

The process of invention has gone on steadily and surely. The rise of the electric-power industry, the spreading use of the internal-combustion engine, and wireless transmission of power have "quickened travel and transportation, spread new arteries for the distribution of goods, and brought backward places within the grasp of urban modes and manners." While the domestic market in terms of population has not grown so rapidly since 1890 as before, it has increased tremendously in the complexity and variety of its wants. The developing network of business communication and contact has spread urban market wants and market usages into the small towns and rural communities of the nation.

Nevertheless, in spite of higher standards of living and larger amounts of purchasing power in the hands of the public, there are signs that the country's industrial capacity *can* catch up with the market demand for goods and even pass it. Since 1899 physical production has increased far more rapidly than population, and total energy has grown precisely twice as fast as population.[29] The steadily advancing machine technique, the development of superorganization, of management, of engineering, and of equipment efficiency have resulted in speeding up industrial growth and production. The shoe began to pinch in 1907-1913. Buying power did keep pace with increased producing power. Because there had been such an increase in production, it was necessary that there should be an increased buying power. The credit structure of the country had to be enlarged. A sound expan-

sion of credit was made possible by the passage
of the Federal Reserve Act in 1913. A more questionable expansion of buying power came to the
rescue of mass production with the development
of instalment buying. In 1914 the war brought
to American production that greatest of economic gifts—"a sellers' market." But it was a
speculators' market, and in it there was no attempt to relate production to consumption, nor
to the purchasing power of the ultimate con-
sumer. People bought everything they could,
contracted with manufacturers for products
which they hoped to sell and not to use. The
bubble burst with the crash of the stock market
in October, 1919, and the "long arctic night" of
1919-1921 set in. The liquidation of inventories
began and the machinery of production came
almost to a stop.

Faced with the new practise of hand-to-mouth
buying and with decreasing purchasing power,
business struggled once more to set the factory
wheels in motion. In 1921 began the period of
high-pressure sales methods, and of generous and
effective advertising. The new principle of
"obsolescence" replaced the old principle of
"wear," and the technique of shortening the
style-life of products was emphasized and extended. The growth of instalment buying to an
annual amount of between five and eight billions of dollars converted future earning power

into current purchasing power. Europe's industry was seriously crippled by the war, and her needs beckoned to American productive capacity. Once more business and industry ran smoothly on to peaks of profit.

It is only recently that the need of relating production to consumption has again been borne in upon the alert. Intensive and extensive marketing necessarily costs money and may even overbalance savings in production. The problems of waste in selling, of more accurate market appraisals, and more scientific calculations of buying power are beginning to raise their ugly heads. European industry is reviving. Domestic competition is increasing the necessity of attending to total costs and not merely to production costs. A steady growth in holding companies, mergers, and amalgamations is still further altering the structure of business. To meet the danger of unlimited competition within a limited market and to gain the physical and pecuniary advantages of large-scale production and large-scale marketing, business is evolving new forms of combination, hitherto undreamed of in their possibilities of size and intricacy. The Industrial Revolution is still under way! As yet there can be no finality to the pattern or the extent of business economy.

Such is the brief and all-too-inadequate chronological story of the development of business economy. All of the many parts have contributed to our present whole—the commutation of feudal dues into money payments, the commutation of labor and commodity rents into money, the rise of crafts, the growth of the town as a trading center, the search for new trade routes and the Commercial Revolution, the program of colonial expansion, the organization of joint-stock companies, the development of banking, the adoption of accounting control, the creation of special organizations for investment and speculation, the establishment of retail shops, the Agricultural Revolution, the rapidity of invention, the shift of power from promoters and operators to directors of capital accumulations, the steady advance in power and energy, the extension of mass production, the development of high-pressure marketing, the growth of instalment buying, the leaping strides of industrial combination.[30] The end is not yet. Change is the rule even of this moment. The business economy travels into the future on the virile and ingenious roads of yesterday and to-day.

V

INFANCY, ADOLESCENCE, AND MATURITY

IF CHRONOLOGY were the most important consideration in the evolution of business economy, the preceding chapters on ancient; medieval, and modern business economies would suffice as background knowledge for a study of the present. But time is not the essential factor which determines the generic processes in the development of business economy.

Not all who lived in the age of Pericles enjoyed the benefits of Athenian business economy. Within six hundred miles of the Athenian market-place, both north and south, there lived peoples who subsisted as tho the world had not advanced beyond prehistoric days. In the thirteenth century, often called the greatest of centuries, when northern Italy was demonstrating to the world how much genius God could infuse into the souls of her sons, there were primitive tribes, even in Europe, thousands of years behind in their modes of acquiring a living.[1] Today, in the twentieth century, we can find peoples in Papua,[2] East Australia, East and West Africa, and Siberia, whose system of economy appears to antedate that of any of the tribes of recorded history. A trip through parts of Europe

in the present year serves to press home the
fact that many villages are still "medieval" in
economy as well as in architecture, costume, and
the "finer aspects of culture." The interior
peoples of China employ the same devices of
livelihood as were typical of fifteenth-century
Europe. In point of economy the Eskimo trails
the ancient Babylonian. So far as time is concerned, the evolution of modern business economy has been far from uniform, anything but
strictly chronological. Some peoples seem not to
have lifted their economies one iota beyond
those of the savages, some have advanced a
hundred years, and still others a thousand or
two.

Nor has geography been any more important as a determinant or as a basic calculator.
"In origin, the terms East and West are mere
references to the dawning sun and its dusky
resting-place." [3] Where the adolescent economies of Java, Central Africa, and Yucatan once
flourished, we now have little to suggest that
those economies might have been hereditary
products of particular areas. Tabriz presented a
more complicated business economy in the fourteenth century than it does to-day, in spite of
the fact that its astronomy has hardly changed.

No doubt a meticulous scholar can discover
many fine points of distinction between the feudalism of Japan and that of medieval Europe,

but for practical purposes the substance of the two orders was the same; the fighting men held the same supremacy in both geographical areas.[4]

At the moment, nearly every national area has its centers of large-scale industry and trade, its sections of infant business economy, and perhaps even its sections of barter economy.

Consequently, in order to supplement and complete our background, some description of the stage-by-stage development of economy is necessary. Only by excluding chronology and geography in large degree, can we, in the purely genetic sense, view the evolution of systems of economy from the simple to the complex.

The most important stages in the evolution of systems of economy are designated somewhat as follows: collectional economy, nomadic economy, settled village economy, town economy, and metropolitan economy. From the point of view of the state of production in these various stages, the sequence is sometimes listed as follows: the stage of direct appropriation, the stage of animal husbandry, the stage of agriculture, the stage of specialized handicraft, and the stage of large-scale power manufacture. These stages are presented in the order of their progress from the simple to the complex. Each succeeding stage denotes an increased complexity over and beyond its predecessor.

The simplest modes of acquiring a living are not concerned with agriculture, as many ordinarily suppose. All the available records indicate that the crude savage did not and does not sustain life by the cultivation of his fields.[5] The writings of the hunters and the explorers who have in our times returned from regions where man lives in a simple state attest the same fact. The Eskimo, for example, fits into this category. The ancient Hindus [6] whom Herodotus described, the Germans [7] of the days of Tacitus, the Veddahs of Ceylon when they were visited by Robert Knox in 1681, and the Shoshone Indians of California present the same general picture. In spite of differences of thousands of years in time and of thousands of miles of distance, all lived in the same stage and according to the same system—variously called the stage of direct appropriation or the system of collectional economy.

These names are apt and precise because these peoples merely collect or appropriate the products of the earth and waters. The woods and the fields are full of animals which can be killed and used for food, clothing, and shelter. The rivers abound in fish and seals. The trees bear fruits and nuts, and along the ground wild vegetables thrive and grow. It is possible to live in simple comfort by merely cutting down and carrying home what Nature provides so bountifully.

There is no organized production. Direct appropriation of Nature's bounties goes on with no effort to modify or increase her gifts. At first, only natural shelters are used and there is no clothing. As more efficient methods of hunting are developed, the use of animals' skins for clothing, for shelters, and for utensils is made possible.

The geographical distribution of animals, the climate, the amount of rainfall, the altitude, and similar factors determine what and how much can be collected or appropriated. Thus the locust-eaters of the Arabian peninsula lived almost entirely on their "flying grain-fields," as these droves of winged insects have sometimes been called. These peoples built huge fires in the caves and narrow ravines. The ascending smoke suffocated the flying insects and caused them to fall by the thousands into the caverns below. Once gathered, the locusts were pulverized and made into cakes.[8] On the Pacific Coast of North America, the Indians lived almost entirely on fish and game. The natives of Western India depended upon vegetables and rice for subsistence. About the Arctic Circle, the Eskimos avail themselves of a varied diet— fish, seal, walrus, polar bear, musk ox and fox. Niggard as these diets seem to us, they are more than sufficient to sustain life. They build hardy men and women.

Direct appropriation necessitates a wandering existence. Relying on the gifts of Nature for food, clothing, and shelter always and inevitably subjects simple man to the whims of Nature. The winds, the rains, and the snows determine the amount of fruits and nuts on the trees, the abundance or lack of vegetables in the ground, and the number and kind of the wild animals in the forests. Currents and tides control the quantities of fish in the coastal waters. When a particular district ceases to yield enough to supply human needs, the collectional man wanders about in search of a district that will so provide. Even as the animals trek northward or southward in search of better feeding grounds, he, too, wanders with them. Improvident and totally unmindful of the value of storage, he is largely dependent upon the animals and the productive lands. If, in his wandering, he finds only barren districts, he starves as do the animals.

There are no masters of hoarded wealth in this system of economy or stage of direct appropriation. No man has more than his needs. Property rights are only vague imaginings and wild dreams. As among the animals of the forest, the strong take from the weak. Indeed, collectional man in his existence is not far removed from the mode of the beasts which he hunts. Even as they, he eats what Nature produces. Even as they, he searches for food and partakes of it until his appetite is satisfied. Even as they, he fears what he does not understand and lives in constant dread of the unusual.

Many economists have refused to consider these modes of acquiring a living as representative of any forms of economy. Such conditions so closely resemble animal existence that many thinkers are wont to hold that they precede the advent of economy. But this opinion is scarcely valid. From its derivation the word "economy" means the system of the household, the regulation of the family. The collectional man has a family. He has a household, even tho he may lack a house. He trades with other men, simple as his trading is. It may be a skin in exchange for a wife, a weapon for a handful of nuts, or even a fur for an ornament. He has his own particular mode of existence. Crude as it is, it seems to deserve the name of economy.

Frequently, accidents are responsible for the development of more complicated customs and practises. When, how, or why some people lift themselves above the stage of direct appropriation is unknown. It may be that they succeed in connecting the dropping of a pit with the subsequent appearance of a tree, and then project just a little beyond. It may be that a cow, captured alive and kept to be killed a little later, gives birth to a calf and thus the idea of animal husbandry dawns. However and whatever the stimulus, it remains a fact that man takes the step from what is called the system of collectional economy to the more complicated system of nomadic economy, to the more productive stage of animal husbandry.

In this stage, hunting, fishing, and the gathering of fruits, nuts, and wild vegetables continue as in the simpler order. But man, instead of merely searching for and collecting Nature's bounties, begins to aid Nature in their production and preservation. In place of eating all the wild vegetables within reach, man returns portions of some to the earth for purposes of production. He sows seed with the thought of a future harvest. He now keeps in captivity the animals he formerly hunted only when the need arose. By their breeding, he assures himself of a continual supply of flesh. He has goats, sheep, and swine, which follow him wherever he wanders. Or to put it more precisely, he follows them. For in this stage man's temporary habitat depends more upon the amount of food available for his animals than upon his own geographical preferences.

What little agriculture is carried on in this stage is crude, haphazard and unimportant. A nomadic life is never conducive to large harvests. The whole process of cultivation is wasteful. The ground is seldom tilled. If weeds spring up to choke the growth, they flourish and spread in unchecked luxuriance. The men rarely engage in planting. The women alone are responsible for any work that is done in the fields.

It is more important to the nomadic man that the animals be captured and domesticated than that the grain be stored. The animals provide meat, milk, clothing, and sheltering tents. Their teeth, horns, and bones can be made into ornaments and utensils. Moreover, the herds and the flocks are more easily protected than cultivated fields or well-stored granaries. At the threatening approach of an enemy man can move his herds to safety, but not his fields and their produce.

Naturally, even the efforts at animal husbandry are makeshift and simple. The breeding of the animals is carried on with no thought of any improvement of the strain. Survival of the fit is the rule of the herd and enforced hardships are many. It is necessary for the herd to wander on driven marches day after day, to be satisfied with scanty fodder and with little or no water. The whole methodology of husbandry is rough and fallow.

The significant change from the stage of direct appropriation is that man becomes provident.

He begins to look forward to future days with the notion of the hunger and the thirst that they may bring. He attempts to preserve breeding animals and to some extent germinating seeds.

Bartering, too, continues with slightly more thought of the productive value of goods to be bargained for in the process. If a man possesses more cattle than he cares to tend, he exchanges several head for a slave whom he puts to work cultivating the fields. If a man needs more women for the planting, he barters whatever he can part with for them.

At the advent of the white man on this continent, many of the North American Indians were living this nomadic existence. To be sure, the men-folk were hunters rather than herders, but the women-folk cultivated maize and corn in the fields. The Hebrews of the post-Egyptian period were mainly nomadic in their economy. They depended upon their flocks more than upon their fields. The Goths and the Huns were living in this stage when they descended upon Europe from the north. The Kelts who left Gaul and became the progenitors of the English were nomads as late as the fifth century B. C. The Greeks passed beyond this stage before the time of Homer. However, many of the tribes in the hinterland of Algeria [9] have gone beyond their nomadic existence only within the last century.

the fields do not yield enough fodder, the animals are driven off to better pastures. Such is the practise in Tibet to-day. The cattlemen who live on the mountainsides begin moving down into the valleys at the approach of winter. By midwinter they are down in the lowlands, and there they remain until the sprouting grass on the mountainsides invites them home again.

Hunting also continues, but gradually loses its importance as the chief means of securing food. Fighting, too, persists to occupy much of the attention of the men. The Welsh of Owen Glendower's days and the Irish at the time of Strongbow's incursion practised the settled-village modes. These peoples left the field work to the women. There was sufficient fighting to occupy the men-folk from one end of the year to the other. The Indian villages in North America, described by the explorers and colonizers of New England and upper New York, also typify the settled-village economy. In this instance, also, hunting was not relegated to the background as a means of providing food. The Indian brave engaged in hunting almost continually: he left the cultivation of the corn, maize, and millet to the squaws. Unlike their fellow men on the other side of the Atlantic, these American redskins never became herders. They domesticated only dogs. All the other animals were the prey of the hunt.

The life of the settled village brings in its wake the serious evil of disease. In nomadic economy man leaves his accumulations of filth behind him as he moves on to new locations. He is scarcely long enough in one spot to suffer any ill effects of his unsanitary habits. But in the settled village man must breathe the air and drink the water which he pollutes. Inevitably, the mortality rate in the settled-village stage is extremely high. Whole villages are denuded of people by typhus. With but the rudiments of medical knowledge, man can fight disease only with his native and God-given strength of body.

Inevitably, the peoples of those villages which are widely separated from the customary trails of wandering pillagers, or whose fortifications are highly impregnable, begin to use the time no longer needed to defend their homes and possessions, in the pursuit of economic improvement. Man commences to pay more attention and to give more effort to the cultivation of the fields. Coarse grains are grown as winter feed for the cattle, to supplement the scanty herbage of the frosts. Grains, vegetables, and fruit are cultivated for use. The principle of land-resting permeates the mind of men. Acreage is allowed to lie fallow or is turned over to grazing at intervals between periods of use for tillage. Agriculture holds full sway, and the domesticated animals are put to its work. Oxen pull out the tree-stumps and the large stones. They haul the simple plow. The cattle manure the fields. The goats clear the ground for planting by the simple process of eating everything that happens to be under their hoofs and noses.

Because grains must be cooked before they are eaten, the art of cookery develops. Wool is spun. Garments are made of cotton, linen, or silk, depending upon the geographical environment of the village. Homes are furnished and various utensils are used for cooking and storing food. "The important fact that homes are settled means that possessions can accumulate— a great incentive to consumption." [10]

It is in this agrarian stage that feudalism usually develops when it visits a certain people. The weaker and more exposed villages turn to some powerful chieftain for protection against the sporadic attacks of wandering tribes, so that steady economic progress may continue. Such villages can ill afford to be squeamish about notions of liberty. They give their fealty willingly to anyone who is strong enough to ward off the attacks of the predatory strangers. In return for the security promised by a powerful lord or baron, the villagers give to him a certain amount of their time and effort. They till his fields, tend his flocks, and repair the fortifications about his castle. They help to feed and maintain their protecting chief or lord and his personal retainers.

Gradually, an important economic change is effected. Instead of receiving all the benefits of their personal labors, many villagers pass on a part to a new class of non-producers. Nevertheless, security is so important, that the villagers count it worth a day's work each week or even more. Man is no longer free. The entering wedge of feudalism comes into his life. The interests of his overlord are not sharply confined to the amelioration of the condition of his village life. Still, new and somewhat beneficial institutions appear in this process of exchange of obligations. Courts develop, and instead of settling village disputes by might, man takes his grievances to his court. The overlord or chief is judge and jury. The court supplants the family feuds.

And so the settled-village economy becomes the antithesis of nomadic life. Feudalism matures and molds its institutions. The villagers cannot leave their lands when they wish. They cannot divide or sell their fields without their lord's consent. In many districts the lords and chiefs by right of might sequester part of the village property as their own, and the villagers with their land become possessions of the master.

Unjust as these conditions seem, they are certainly responsible for more intensive cultivation of the fields. The commoner who cannot leave his

land makes it produce as much as possible. He
learns to store his foodstuffs. He realizes that
the size of his fields limits the number of animals he can keep. He slaughters, smokes, and
stores his excess.

Because of the limitations of their fields, some
of the subject-villagers find it necessary to eke
out a living for their families by supplementing cultivation with manufacturing activities.
In leisure moments they begin to fabricate tools,
pitchers, baskets, shoes and clothes for purposes
of exchange. Those who find themselves apt at
building repair their neighbors' huts in exchange for measures of wheat. However, there is
little division of labor, and these tasks are leisure
tasks rather than specialized occupations. For
the most part every family makes its own consumption goods. If specialized occupations appear, they are usually concerned with facilitat-
ing the making of productive goods. In most
cases the office of a blacksmith or tool-maker is
the first industrial occupation.[11]

Haphazard bartering continues. Goods are exchanged for goods, a hide for wheat, a pair of
boots for a crude ax, a goat for a plow, and so
on. "Intramural" trade is the only trade, because the whole village remains self-sufficient.

Complex as it is, the settled-village economy is
not destined to remain the highest form of econ-

omy. The agrarian type of production soon
emerges into the stage of specialized handicraft.
Very quickly, many of the village communities
grow beyond themselves. Locations on the sea-
shore, the river bank, the main highway or
caravan route, change the village from an agricultural to a commercial unit. As the village
grows in population, wants increase in amount
and variety. Family self-sufficiency becomes difficult. The so-called division of labor begins.
It becomes evident that a man who is a shoe-
maker six days a week succeeds in turning out
a better pair of boots than the farmer who turns
cobbler but one day a month. The former villager who inclines towards craftsmanship gives
up his cultivation and drifts away from the village and into the town. The villager who inclines more towards cultivation than towards
craftsmanship begins to give up his attempt to
supply all the needs of his household by the work
of his hands, devotes a larger share of his time
to his fields, and depends upon the town for
many of his consumption goods.

During this stage there may be at first something of a tendency for groups to specialize in
some particular form or forms of production,
"as the Greeks specialized in fine arts, the early
modern English in woolen textiles, the Chinese
in paper and pottery." [12] Nevertheless, the town,
as such, is still pretty much self-sufficient. Every

needed task finds willing specialists, who work in their homes and sometimes even in establishments "such as the factories for the production of pottery, the ruins of which have been found in Greece."[13] Better boots, better clothing, better carts, better farm implements become the handicraft ideal.

Men begin to specialize in buying and selling as well. Definite retailing locations are established. Designated produce markets, which are indicated by the "market cross," appear. Commodity money and coined money are more widely used. Instead of going to the farm for vegetables, to the herder for lambs, or to the seacoast for fish, man depends upon his visits to established and specialized retail markets, the vegetable stand, the butcher shop, and the fish mart. Middlemen thus commence to break away from cultivation and fabrication and make subsistence profits in commodity or coined money which may be used to secure family necessities. In fact, one of the chief points of difference between the agricultural village and the commercial town is that the latter houses many non-producers in the sense of cultivation or fabrication. Many men become mere handlers who buy from all and sell to all.

Various sections and streets of the growing towns are finally commandeered by particular industries. The hosiers, the drapers, the goldsmiths, and the fishdealers localize their places of business. The proximity of location and the identity of occupation unites the handicrafts and also the tradesmen. Craft and merchant gilds develop for purposes of mutual protection.

For the proper development of handicraft and trading the town needs more freedom than the settled village. Accordingly, wherever feudalism exists, in the process of transforming the village into the town, there is a constant effort to procure more privileges from the lord or abbot master. The struggle for freedom usually culminates in a grant of freedom secured by threat, actual revolt, or purchase. Economically, the town becomes independent of a feudal overlord.

For a time it attempts to work out the ideal of town self-sufficiency, but before long it realizes its dependence upon the surrounding countryside and upon the production of other towns near by and far away. An increasing use of coined money in trading, a developing emphasis upon money-profits, a continuing expansion of town-production, and a rapid growth in the variety of man's wants completely break down the ideal of town self-sufficiency. Local barriers fall with a crash as business men reach out in search of money-profits. Roads are improved, bridges are constructed, and rivers are deepened. The process of linking town to town goes on apace to prepare the way for a still more complicated economy.

The rapidly-growing town soon comes to be known as a metropolis. This term originally meant "mother-city" and was used to designate a city whose sons had founded other towns or cities. Tyre was thus the mother-city of Carthage, and Troy of Rome. As the years rolled on, the meaning of the word changed, and metropolis came to be used in the sense of "chief city," a large city surrounded by smaller cities and towns which depend upon it and use it as a central agency for trade.

The kind of economy that is characteristic of the metropolis is vastly more complicated than that of the town. As population increases and people pile "high up on one another in cities," business organization and technique are rapidly elaborated and expanded. To provide the physical goods necessary to the life and comfort of "an increasing mass of landless, toolless, and homeless people dependent upon the caprices of trade" is an enormous task. Wholesaling as a business enterprise assumes an immediate importance. Merchants must buy and keep in stock large quantities and wide varieties of all commodities.

The necessity for carrying produce into the metropolis and for distributing some of it out of the metropolis again to the dependent towns and villages brings into being the "common carrier." It is no longer profitable for each merchant to own and operate his own ships and wagons. Transportation becomes a specialized activity and entreats inventive genius to furnish motive power. The winding and narrow streets of the town give way to broad, paved thoroughfares. Attention is turned to communication with dependent towns and other metropolitan centers.

Steam soon comes to the city, and the era of large-scale power manufacture is born. The machine age dawns upon the city, and sets up a new stage of production. The machine is thought out before it is made. It is a specialist. It is a fast and continuous worker. It is capable of concentrating energy. And it is independent of human energy. The first results of manufacturing by power machinery are the breakdown of domestic handicraft, and the concentration of population in the cities because the workers must live near their factories. "Steam culture demands great, roaring cities." [14] Workers forsake their farms and drift into the city factories. Women and children leave the home and accept employment in the mills. A staggering amount and an amazing variety of machine-made goods pour forth from the city factories to be transported to the ends of the earth. The specialization of labor continues, but there is even more specialization by machines. As a result, goods are produced far more quickly and cheaply than ever.

Man becomes increasingly dependent on the city and its public activities. There is danger from impure food which passes through the hands of many middlemen. Weights and measures must be inspected. New health problems arise. The control of vice and crime presents a perplexing and costly social question. Fire hazards spring up on every side. Streets must be better paved, lighted, and policed. New means of transit must be provided.[15]

The individual loses his economic self-sufficiency and independence. He becomes an employee. He no longer owns his tools or even his home. His daily life is regulated by the clock and the whistle. His work is highly specialized. His home is often merely a cheaper rooming place than can be had elsewhere. If he can "count his change," pull a lever, and "recognize a delicatessen store" when he sees one, he can survive in the city with far fewer skills than can the primitive man in the stage of direct appropriation.[16]

One and all must live by making and spending money, for the city suddenly becomes minutely specialized in production and marketing. The business or money-profits economy comes of age.

As the smoke rises, we find a surprizing new phenomenon—the cardinal importance of cash. . . . A farmer with a loom in his house is not primarily dependent on cash. He needs a little of it every year, but he can feed and clothe his family without it. A mechanic in an automobile factory, a shopgirl in a department store, can hardly get through the day without money. A cashless week may find them starving. No part of their daily labor provides them with consumable goods. They do not make anything which they can eat or wear. Edibles and wearables can only be secured with the money which must first be found. Invariably this leads to the enthronement of money as the most important thing in life. As indeed it is in a specialized economy: as indeed it is not in the ultimate scale of human values."

And then, just at the moment when "the belching smokestack" is generally accepted as the symbol of the city, new sources of power arise. Electricity and the gas engine knock at the door of the city, and announce themselves as willing "to emancipate mankind from utter dependence upon the fixed plant and railway."[18] Electric power begins to distribute its magic force to shop, loft (the city's new manufacturing establishment), and home. It even transmits power in any quantity to the surrounding rural districts. The gas-engined trucks spread out over a new network of paved arteries, even unto the lowliest general store at the crossroads.

With amazing rapidity the motor-truck and then the commercial airplane "break down the barriers recently erected between city and country by the steam engine, checking the rate of concentration in the great municipalities and strengthening the economy of the small town." [19] Aided by power and the machine, the basic principles of mass production—the making of standard interchangeable parts and the assembling of these parts into the completed unit with a minimum of handicraft labor—are applied on an ever increasing scale.[20] Aided by power and the machine, the principles of mass distribution—branch warehousing, sale by description through ultimate-consumer advertising, and even automatic retail vending—also are applied to distribute the flood of goods. Metropolitan trading customs, metropolitan goods, and metropolitan financial practises spread out over the entire country and into its every "nook and cranny."

We are clearly living at the present moment in the stage of large-scale power manufacture under an advanced business or money-profits metropolitan economy, which is gaining ground in all quarters of the globe and in every section of our nation. When we look back upon the enormous increase in the electrification of industry, the rise of the Diesel engine, the astounding multiplication of international cables, the bewildering growth of the radio, and the stupendous advancement of aviation, and then peer forward into the future to vision an airport on every other roof, we hesitate indeed to tag our next step with any definite name. We can only presume that the more complicated stages to come will retain most of the present fundamental essentials of a business or money-profits economy.

VI

THE BUSINESS ENTERPRISE

Some unit of organization is necessary to furnish the initiating urge, the consistent driving power, and the guiding direction for the performance of society's "business" tasks. The process of making and spending money involves all the many and varied institutions of production, exchange, and distribution. It calls for an effective coordination of the factors of labor, capital, and brain. Even in the simplest business undertaking there is need for some unit of organization to vitalize the complicated activities of the whole endeavor.

In our present business or money-profits economy the characteristic and dominant unit of organization for *making* money is the business enterprise. The origin of the term harks back to the old English word "enterpriser," commonly applied to the "adventurer" who embarked in the uncertain argosies of foreign trade. In current usage, however, *business enterprise* has taken unto itself a precise and definite meaning. "A business enterprise is an organization which seeks to realize pecuniary profits upon an investment of capital, by a series of transactions concerned with the purchase and sale of goods in terms of money."[1] The "transactions" of the business enterprise may, in fact, be the execution of any one or of any combination of the following functions: fabricating, assembling (buying), distributing (selling), storing, sorting and grading, traffic control, financing and risk-taking. The "goods" in which the business enterprise may deal may be "commodities of any vendible kind" from spats to pig-iron, functional services of execution, technical advice, or even "rights" such as bank credit, securities, or insurance.

The chief incentive of an adventuring business enterprise is, of course, the desire for profits. It is possible to think of economic enterprises as owned by the government and operated by commissions, as owned by the government and operated by committees of workers, as owned by the government and operated by "some elected despot."[2] But in our present business or money-profits economy, business enterprises are owned and operated by individuals or collections of individuals. According to the laws of private property, the fruits of their ownership and of their operation of business enterprises belong to them. These fruits or profits furnish the incentive to business undertakings.

In any high development of a business or money-profits economy, production comes to be carried on by the business enterprise rather than by the family. Exceptions, of course, persist as continuations of earlier economic orders. The domestic work of housewives, the farm production of produce for home consumption, the cultivation of vegetables in family gardens, the leasing of farm land by tenants who pay as rent a share of the crops—these are productive concerns of the family. In such survivals of exchange by barter, the family is still the dominant unit of organization. Generally speaking, however, the family has been definitely superseded by the business enterprise as the dominant unit of organization for *making* money.[3] The business enterprise coordinates the efforts of a number of individuals drawn from several or many families. It pays each individual a money-income and consciously coordinates his efforts with the efforts of several or multitudes of others.

Every individual who is working on his own account, whether he be farmer, lawyer, pedler, newsboy, certified public accountant, author, or what-not, may be classified as an "enterpriser." Such an individual obtains a money-income by buying and selling goods or by selling his services. However, these individual and small-scale business enterprises are few in number and are scarcely typical of "business" in our present money-profits economy. In general, they are sharply confined to farming, the professions, personal service, repair work and petty trade. In all probability the number of men working on their own account did not exceed 11,000,000 in 1920.[4] These small-scale business enterprises have been pushed into the background by the growth of corporate ownership and large-scale production. Altho the small business enterprise rests upon the same basic feature of modern economy as does the large-scale enterprise, namely, the private ownership of tools, the small-scale business enterprise differs in broad essentials. "In commercial alertness and business method, in complexity or organization, in dependence upon the money market, the typical farm, repair shop, neighborhood store, and boarding-house are in a different class from the enterprises typical of mining, manufacturing, commerce and finance."[5]

The characteristic business enterprise of the present is the large-scale business enterprise. In manufacturing, statistics show us that in 1921, less than 3 per cent. of our plants turned out more than 59 per cent. of our total manufactured products. About 20 per cent. of our plants produced more than nine-tenths of our total manufacturing output. The manufacturing map of the moment is that of a network of enormous factories under corporate ownership and operation, rather than a map merely dotted here and there with "isolated plants owned by natural persons engaged in competitive production to meet local needs."[6] In the fields of railway and marine transportation, large-scale business enterprises have a sway which is almost complete. In mining, lumbering, construction, warehousing, wholesaling, insurance, and banking, the large-scale enterprise is the dominant enterprise, altho it is not the sole performer of business activity. To a somewhat lesser degree, it is also important in retailing, journalism, fishing, market-gardening, hotel keeping, and in the various and several amusement fields. Of late, too, the pecuniary advantages of large-scale business enterprise have been widely sought in dairying, fruit-raising, general farming, and even in many of the so-called learned professions—engineering, law, medicine, education, and architecture.[7]

In any quest for profits the array of advantages offered by large-scale operation is imposing and enticing. It is small wonder that modern business men in their efforts to play first fiddle in competition and to secure the economies of large-scale operations have made the large business enterprise the characteristic unit of the times.

Developing forms of external organization have made large-scale enterprises possible. So far as form is concerned, society allows individuals and collections of individuals to organize business enterprises in a number of different ways. Law is perhaps our strongest and most definite form of control, so that it is not surprizing that the law is used to a large extent in defining what each form of business enterprise is so far as its organization is involved and in stating what each form may or may not do.

The oldest and simplest form of organization is the individual proprietorship. This type of organization existed long before any name was applied to it, and even to this day it is governed very largely by common law, altho many statutes also limit and define an individual proprietor's relationship with others. While it is true that many companies that employ thousands of workers and use thousands of dollars of capital have grown up under the direction and control of single individuals, this form of organization is commonly used by small manufacturers, by professional men, by small retailers, and by farmers. In this type of organization, unhampered power is concentrated in the hands of one individual. The proprietor is his own master, but generally his kingdom is a small one, and rarely does it extend beyond his immediate neighborhood. The limitations of this form of organization are many. In the first place, there is a limit to the amount of capital one man may command as compared with what may be secured by a number of men. Again, an individual may need more help than he can secure from paid employees and may attempt to carry too much upon his

THE BUSINESS ENTERPRISE

own shoulders. A great risk is involved where so much depends upon the health and life of an individual proprietor. Moreover, in case of failure, the individual proprietor's whole personal fortune is at stake. All his assets, over and above any amount he has put into his enterprise, may be called upon to pay his creditors. Because of these limitations, individual proprietorships are often short-lived. They are easy to form and easy to end.

When an individual proprietor feels the need for an associate who will help him bear his business burdens, or when he sees an opportunity of expanding his business by putting up another building, equipping it with more machinery and hiring more men to work for him, he begins to look about for a moneyed friend or acquaintance who may be willing to come into the business as a partner. A partnership is an association of two or more individuals who are jointly and severally liable for the management of the enterprise in which they are engaged. Each partner invests a certain sum, not necessarily equal in amount to that invested by any other partner, and signs a legally-binding contract which states the purpose of the partnership and the rights and duties of the partners. Each partner is liable for the entire debt of the firm. One partner, either stupidly or with criminal intent, may secretly sign a contract that will bring financial losses to the partnership. No matter how much the other partners may protest, the individually-signed contract is binding upon the other partners individually and severally. Then, too, since a partnership is based upon a contract among several persons, the partnership automatically ends when one partner withdraws or dies. A live business is more valuable than a dead one, and the sudden dissolution of a partnership may be very embarrassing and harmful to the remaining partners. Finally, partners cannot be multiplied indefinitely, or too many cooks will spoil the broth.

The joint-stock company is a kind of expanded partnership without some of the disadvantages of an ordinary partnership. This form of organization grew up in England, as has already been noted in Chapter IV. In its basic form it was used in many fields of business until 1862, when Parliament accepted the principle of limited liability of stockholders. In this same basic form it has never been popular in the United States. The joint-stock company divides the capital into shares, and as many persons can take part in the enterprise as there are shares. It is possible, for example, for a company with a capital of $1,000,000 to divide this capital into shares of $100 each and thereby to have as many as 10,000 owners. Even a hundred owners can hardly expect to manage a business jointly as partners, so in a joint-stock company the share-owners elect representatives, according to the regulations of the by-laws, and these representatives (the board of directors) manage the enterprise. In this respect the owners are not partners, for they have no share in the management. In another respect they are partners, for they are responsible for the debts of the company, even with their personal and private assets. Shares may be sold from one person to another without ending the life of the company, so that it is possible for this kind of organization to exist indefinitely.

It seemed hardly fair to our business forefathers that a man who owned only one share in a joint-stock company should be individually liable and responsible for the company's debts. Therefore, they created a new form of company called the limited-liability company. Even before 1800, the ordinary partnership and the joint-stock company form of expanded partnership were recognized as incompletely meeting the needs of a developing business that demanded larger capital funds and a greater certainty of duration. Accordingly, certain States, by statute law, authorized forms of organization still bearing the word "partnership" in their titles but limiting the liability of the partners and making it possible for the enterprises to continue in the event of the death or withdrawal of a particular partner. These special acts of various State legislatures need not concern us here, except that we should note that they indicated a feeling towards the corporate form of organization. Not long after 1800, general laws were passed providing for the establishment of corporate business enterprises.

Corporations are, then, formed under the laws of the several States. At the request of a prescribed number of individuals, and after the performance of certain stipulated formalities, a particular State government creates a corporation by issuing a certificate of incorporation. The formulated corporation is legally an individual, with many of the prerogatives and obligations of an actual person. It may enter into contracts as an individual entity, it may sue in the courts, it may be sued for damages, and it may commit a crime. The capital or money with which it begins and continues its business activities is supplied by persons who receive shares, commonly called stock, in exchange for the cash or other property invested by them in the corporation. These shares give their holders a proportion of the total ownership in accordance with the relative amount of stock owned. An individual may own one share or he may own many. His rights depend upon the number of shares he owns. His principal rights are to help elect the directors who are to manage the affairs of the corporation, and to share in such profits as may be distributed to stockholders. The corporation is managed by the board of directors and such other officers as are employed by the board.

The corporation differs from other forms of business organization in a number of important essentials. It is a permanent organization and continues even tho its promoters die or retire. The transfer of shares from one owner to another has no effect upon its life. Its charter from the State may possibly run only for a limited time, but usually it can be easily renewed. As has been indicated, the liability of each stockholder in the corporation is limited. The individual stockholder is liable only to the amount which he has actually paid in or which he has pledged in return for stock. Beyond this amount he is not liable, no matter how much the corporation may owe. The principal exception to this statement of liability is an incorporated national bank, in which each stockholder is liable for twice the amount of his stock subscription. Finally, there is no limit to the amount of capital a corporation may obtain. This form of organization is particularly well adapted to gather huge amounts of capital from thousands of investors. The possibility of using different types of securities with varying rates of return, and the possibility of issuing these securities in small denominations, makes it easy to reach differing types of investors.

If a corporation makes profits through its business operations, some or all of these profits may be left in the corporation, or some may be distributed to the stockholders. Profits which are left in the business are called *surplus*, to distinguish such amounts from the capital stock originally subscribed. Profits which are distributed to stockholders are called *dividends*. Payments of dividends may be made from accumulated profits but cannot legally be made from the original capital. Dividends may be paid in scrip (an unsecured interest-bearing note), in additional stock, and in property, as well as in cash.

In general, there are two kinds of corporate securities—stocks and bonds. Stocks represent shares in the ownership of the business; bonds represent loans to the corporation.

Frequently, corporations issue *preferred* as well as *common* stocks. When preferred stocks are designated as *preferred as to dividends*, the owners of such stock must receive their dividends out of the first profits earned by the corporation and distributed by the directors, but only up to some previously stated amount—usually from six to eight per cent. If the preferred stock is *non-participating*, the owners of it cannot receive more than the stipulated percentage of its face value, no matter what the owners of common stock may receive.[8] However, if the preferred stock is *participating*, the owner of it may receive a portion of the profits in addition to the stipulated percentage, this additional payment being determined by the percentage of dividend given to a share of common stock or on the basis of some other "ratio which the organizers may have provided." [9] Often the preferred stock is *cumulative*, which means that if preferred dividends are not paid at the stipulated rate in any year or in a number of years, they mount up as a cumulative total and constitute a claim on the corporation's future earnings—a claim that must be paid before the common stockholders can receive any dividends. The owner of preferred stock is still further protected if his stock is *preferred as to assets*. In case of bankruptcy, the holders of such stock are entitled to receive the par value of their stock holdings before the common stockholders can "receive any of the proceeds of the liquidation." [10]

As a rule the control of the management of a corporation is in the hands of the owners of common stock. Voting power is generally given to the common stock, and each share of common stock normally carries with it the right of one vote. Sometimes, in order to keep the voting control in the hands of a small group "without compelling them to own a majority of the whole common issue," the common stock is divided into two classes, A and B, and the voting power is given to one class only. The owner of common stock assumes more risks than the owner of preferred stocks, but if the activities of the corporation are highly profitable, such an owner may receive very much more in dividends and in appreciation of stock value. In many instances the dividends on common stock vary considerably from year to year, but some corporations follow the practise of creating reserves in highly profitable years, so that a steady rate of dividend payment on common stocks can be maintained.

Bonds are also used by corporations to obtain the capital necessary to carry on their activities. They are promises to pay a definite sum of money at some future date and to pay interest upon that sum of money at the rate fixed in the bond. When an individual borrows money on a house, he usually secures the money from an individual person or bank and gives his promissory note with his mortgage. A corporation, however, that borrows millions, gives a mortgage on its property, but splits the total sum of the loan into a large number of separate bonds or notes. Bonds, then, are subdivisions of a large loan, issued in convenient denominations of $100 or $1,000, for example, so that they can be sold to large numbers of people. Bonds are usually secured by specific assets of the corporation. Sometimes they are issued against collateral—other stocks and bonds owned by the company. Often they are simple debenture bonds, constituting merely general claims against the corporation.

One other form of organization of business enterprise which should be mentioned is the cooperative society. Recently the laws of the several States have begun to be adapted to the new form of corporation known as the cooperative association or society, an organization of producers or consumers for joint economic action. An attempt is being made to bring about the adoption of a uniform enabling act for cooperative societies, and already similar laws have been placed on the statute books of about two-thirds of the States. The most important types of cooperative associations or societies are concerned with handling and marketing producers' products, or with cooperative purchasing for consumers, or with cooperative credit.

The aim of the cooperative society is the same as the aim of any other type of business enterprise: it seeks to realize pecuniary profits. Frequently, however, these societies are referred to as "non-profit" organizations. The meaning here is simply that any profits (savings) beyond a moderate return on the invested capital do not remain in the hands of the association or society itself, but go back to those individuals whose patronage created such profits (savings), not as percentage dividends on stock owned, but on some basis commensurate with the volume of business contributed. This is ordinarily accomplished by operating the cooperative association on a deferred-payment basis, which permits withholding from sales or purchases enough money to cover expenses. After all charges are met, including dividends on stock at ordinary interest rates, the balance of the profits (savings) are distributed to the individual members on the basis of the amount of business contributed by each member. Ordinarily, the control of the cooperative association is vested in the members irrespective of the amount of stock that may be owned. This is particularly true of most of the agricultural-marketing cooperative associations, which usually give each shareholder one vote and no more, regardless of the number of shares he may own.

In 1925, the United States Department of Agriculture reported that 10,803 cooperative associations were engaged in the handling and marketing of farm products, with a total membership of about 2,450,000 farmers. Some 1,200 cooperative purchasing associations were also reported among the farmers by the Department. In 1923, some 10,000 building and loan societies— the usual form of the cooperative credit society

—were in existence, with a total membership of nearly seven million persons.[11]

Altho there were but a handful of corporations in existence in the United States a hundred years ago, this form of organization of the business enterprise overshadows all others at the present time. As for mere number, corporations are still outnumbered by individual proprietorships; but with respect to the number of wage-earners employed and the value of the goods or services produced or handled, the corporation leads all the rest. In 1920, corporations owned 32 per cent. of all American manufacturing establishments, employed 87 per cent. of the wage-earners, and turned out 88 per cent. of the value produced. In mining, corporations owned 51 per cent. of the mines, employed 94 per cent. of the wage-earners, and produced 94 per cent. of the product. In transportation, corporations did 95 per cent. of the work. Farming reported 12,376 existing corporations, retailing (not including department stores) reported 50,604, domestic service reported 7,298, amusements reported 5,258 and the so-called "professions" reported 10,510. In all probability, the corporation to-day performs between 50 and 60 per cent. of the total work of American business.

The prevalence of corporate organization has made it easy for business enterprises to follow the path of group development. It is hardly surprizing that combinations of single business enterprises are growing so rapidly, for business leadership is increasingly seeking those large-scale "elements of strength and security that express themselves in economies and profits."

Combinations of business enterprises have been built up in the main by five different methods: simple agreements, pools, trusts proper, holding companies, and outright consolidations.

The "gentlemen's agreement" is the simplest form of business combination. The various executive officers of a number of single business enterprises merely enter into an informal agreement on matters of common concern. No formal papers are signed by any party to the agreement. Such agreements often involve promises not to invade a rival's territory, not to cut below certain prices in competition, not to expand production facilities, and not to approach a certain group of prospective buyers. These agreements are hard to detect, but usually they are short-lived, because they depend entirely on the extent to which each member abides by his pledge. In the early history of the iron, steel, and anthracite-coal industries, it was a commonplace statement that there was more "honor among thieves than among these makers of gentlemen's agreements." [12]

The so-called pool is another form of early business combination. A pool is formed by drawing up—among the executives of a number of competing business enterprises—a pooling agreement not to compete with each other. Each signing company retains its own identity, but agrees to turn over to a central organization or Board of Control the power to establish the total output for the ensuing year and the power to allot to individual members of the pool certain sharing percentages of the total output. Pools have been annual agreements, in the main. In most cases they have been ineffective, because of individual infractions of the agreement. In 1890, pools were made illegal by the Sherman Anti-Trust Law.

The first "trust" was formed in 1879 as the Standard Oil Company. For purposes of control, about thirty different business enterprises were gathered together under a board of trustees who held the stocks of the several enterprises in a trust relationship. These trustees received the stock of each shareholder in each of the thirty combining enterprises, and issued to each shareholder a trust certificate. Since the trustees then held the stock in the original companies they had the power to operate the combined concerns as a unit, to declare dividends, etc. During the decade following 1879, many hundred trusts were organized. Much popular opposition to the trust soon developed, for people felt that its objects were to create monopolies, to stifle competition, and to raise prices. Many States passed anti-trust statutes of different kinds, and in 1890 the Sherman Anti-Trust Act made illegal any combination which lessens competition or is, in the legal phrase, "in restraint of trade." In June, 1890, the New York State Circuit Court of Appeals declared the North River Sugar Refining Company, a "trust," to be illegal on the ground that a corporation must be controlled by its directors in the interests of its stockholders and that its directors cannot "delegate their powers to trustees or serve others than their own stockholders." [13]

Very quickly after the trust proper was judged illegal a new form of combination appeared—the holding company. Corporations were formed with the stated purpose of acquiring and owning all or a majority of stock in a number of business enterprises. This form of organization was legal, for the holding company does what it is incorporated by the State to do. Nevertheless, while the form of this combination is legal, the activities of such a combination are subject to check under the Sherman Act, the Clayton Act, and other anti-trust laws.

The development of the holding or parent company, the creation of financial alliances between independent enterprises by an exchange of stocks, and the consolidation of independent enterprises, have all gone on with amazing rapidity and have wondrously entangled financial relationships among business enterprises.

The desire to control preliminary or subsidiary processes has resulted in what is called the vertical consolidation, the combining or "integrating" of the various enterprises that are engaged in the production of a product, from the raw-material stage to the stage of finished goods. This kind of consolidation combines enterprises that operate at different stages. A shoe-manufacturing company, for example, may integrate backward and acquire tanneries, or it may integrate forward and acquire retail shoe stores. Either or both processes of integration will produce a vertical consolidation. The desire to control output and prices within a given market results in a horizontal consolidation. Such a consolidation is based upon the elimination of competition and would in all probability at once run counter to the anti-trust laws. A typical horizontal consolidation would be that which included all the automobile plants in the United States. The desire for the economies of large-scale marketing are responsible for the latest type of consolidation, sometimes called circular consolidation. These consolidations appear not to be concerned with acquiring raw-material enterprises or retail stores, nor with eliminating competition. Apparently, their aim is to control a number of non-competing products on the ground that the same salesman who visits the wholesaler or retailer might "as well handle a dozen or score of articles as one."[14] The evolution of the Postum Company into the General Foods Corporation is a good example of this type of consolidation.

Obviously, the principal causes of consolidation—the desire for the economies of large-scale production and large-scale marketing, the desire to control preliminary or subsidiary processes, and the desire to eliminate competition within some market—are vitally powerful factors that will grow in importance as the years roll on.

The day of industrial giants is arriving posthaste. The reasons for industrial combination are so impelling that most of the obstacles to it seem by contrast only molehills to be crushed under the steam-roller of economic inevitability. Economically, consolidation is sound. To the individual owner of business it offers safety and profit. Financially, it has no reasonable limit and can be productive of great profits. Such a triangle of forces presents a solid base indeed for the construction of new giant industrial enterprises.

What the character of the consolidations of the future will be it is not difficult to say. . . . Where competition requires the linking of all of the production and distributing processes, vertical merger will be the rule of the industry. Where competition has reached a dangerous point in profit possibilities, or where size is necessary for increased productive efficiency, horizontal consolidation will be the prevailing type. Where the problem of distribution and the opportunities for profit through the use of highly skilled management suggest industrial integration, circular consolidation will be an outstanding development.[15]

VII

THE RÔLE OF MANAGEMENT

MILLIONS of people have read Elbert Hub-
bard's *Message to Garcia* and have been vitally
stirred by its central thesis. The point of the
story lies in the fact that Rowan accepted his
assignment, shouldered its risks, and carried it
through. Overcoming many difficulties, he found
Garcia and delivered the message. He finished
the task. Had he subscribed to the philosophy
that "it is better to travel hopefully than to
arrive," the story might never have been
written.

The business manager must enter upon his
quest for profits in much the same spirit. Like
Rowan, he must accept his responsibilities willingly and he must see his tasks through.

> He must be a good finisher, for *his task is not
> successful until it has been completed and is
> measured by its results, which should be profits.*
> Of course, as a man in a spiritual way, he may
> have gained greatly by failing; but as a busi-
> ness man, he only gains (and the community
> only gains) by his being a successful finisher.[1]

The survival or extinction of a particular business enterprise is determined by the financial
test of profits. And the primary and major re-

sponsibility for the pecuniary success or failure of a business enterprise rests upon the shoulders of management.

In earlier days, the individual "captalist-employer" was the head of the typical business enterprise. He it was who provided all or a large part of the invested funds, assumed all the hazards, performed "the work of superintendence," and took all the profits. The growth of corporate organization and the spread of large-scale operations have rapidly accomplished a complete separation of management from other functions. At present, for example, the work of management is largely dissociated from ownership.[2] The bulk of corporate funds is furnished by a "miscellaneous and shifting body of stockholders," and by bondholders who may or may not be shareholders in addition. The supervision of the corporation's affairs is turned over to a board of directors, and this board passes the task of management on to a set of general officers who are paid fixed salaries and who may or may not hold a single share of ownership in the corporation. Then, too, the necessity for the coordination of the large numbers of workers and the necessity for the coordination of complicated and highly-specialized processes, both of which are characteristic of large-scale operations, have resulted in the transference of thought, skill, and intelligence from workers to machines and management. The special responsibility for the profit-making operation of the business enterprise is the concern of the salaried general officers of management rather than of a "capitalist-employer."

The "management" of a business enterprise includes the whole sweep of policies and devices by which the internal operations of the enterprise are directed and executed, and by which the external relationships of the enterprise are coordinated with its business and social interests.[3] Even in the case of the external relationships of the business enterprise, management must put its business interests first and its social interests second if there is need for choice. Frequently, however, these two sets of interests coincide, and of late it appears that in order to make money it is more than ever necessary to make goods. Nevertheless, when a choice is necessary, management must subordinate industry to business. "To prosper, even to survive, business enterprises must make profits—not every year, but on the average."[4] Consequently the central and controlling aim of management must be to make profits.

Since profits are made by a connected series of purchases and sales of goods, services, or rights, two fundamental factors or conditions appear to affect the process. The margins between the prices at which goods, services, or rights can be bought and at which these commodities can be sold is certainly one basic factor. Closely connected with price margins is the second basic factor, the present and prospective volume of transactions.

Obviously, then, management is vitally concerned with controlling costs. Wherever and whenever possible, the purchase price (cost) of the commodity in which the business enterprise deals, must be reduced. Nor does this cost mean the manufacturing cost alone, or any other particular functional cost. Management is interested in total costs, because profits or losses are the differences between total costs and the prices obtained in the sale of the enterprise's commodities. Manufacturing costs, marketing costs, and "overhead" costs are all important, since they are component parts of total costs. This necessity for controlling total costs, and for reducing them if possible, confronts the management of any business enterprise, large or small. While an increased volume of transactions presents new opportunities for reducing costs, the basic problem of economical and effective methods and their relation to total costs is always present in the business enterprise, irrespective of the volume of its transactions. Unfortunately, as enterprises grow and as the volume of their transactions increases, total costs are often lost sight of in the glee with which management watches its shrinking manufacturing and overhead costs. Such reductions, of course, are of little avail so far as profits are concerned, if the new and efficient mass-production results in frenzied and wasteful marketing. The cost of finding or creating new markets may completely counterbalance any manufacturing savings brought about by scientific methods of large-scale production. Total costs present the proper internal approach to the problem of making profits.

Generally speaking, it would seem that management has devoted most of its attention to manufacturing costs. For the past fifty years the processes of making goods have been steadily improved, and manufacturing costs have been decreased. In the beginning, American industry was built up on a foundation of abundant raw material, a shortage of labor, and a rapidly growing domestic market hemmed in by walls of protective tariff but containing no tariff barriers within itself. Perhaps it was but natural, then, that management should be wasteful of materials, unconcerned with marketing and saving of labor.

Labor saving involved primarily the use of machinery, and the tremendous development of labor-saving devices in this country was born of the necessity for increasing the productivity of whatever labor was available. As rapidly as possible each step of the industrial process was taken from the hands of the skilled artizan aided by some elementary mechanical apparatus and turned over to the hands of some complicated mechanical device merely aided by an unskilled artizan.[5]

From labor and machinery, management turned to the control of materials—raw, in process, and finished goods. To the problem of marketing and the coordination of manufacturing with marketing all too little thought has yet been given by business management.

Certainly, the first application of the methodology of science to the problem of management was made in the field of manufacturing. In the Midvale Steel Plant, during the eighties, a young engineer named Frederick W. Taylor launched the "scientific management" movement. What Taylor aimed to do was "to apply scientific methodology—as opposed to trial and error—to the job of making up a given amount of raw material into a given finished product, on the principle of a minimum of waste and friction."[6] He hoped, in rough, to influence management to substitute science for guesswork. Perhaps the best definition of his general aims is found in the words of Copley, Taylor's most important biographer:

The grand ends to which this system is all directed may be here defined as (1) the determination of best or standard ways, implements, and materials by scientific investigation and experimentation, and (2) a control so extensive and intensive as to provide for the maintenance of all standards in this way reached.[7]

In seeking these "grand ends" Taylor developed detailed devices and concrete aids, the use of which he widely advocated. Chief among these devices were time study, the use of slide rules, the "differential rate," functional or divided foremanship, instruction cards for workmen, mnemonic systems for classifying goods and implements, the "task" idea accompanied by a cash bonus for the successful performance of the task, the planning room, detailed cost accounting, and a routing system.[8] Any one or any combination of these devices does not, of course, constitute a system of scientific management. The essence of scientific management is rather the fact that it aims to set up a "100 per cent. standard," based upon the *best* way of doing a job as determined by extant technical knowledge and experimental discovery.

Taylor's system of management and the later modifications of his system are justly entitled to the claim of being scientific, because they make definite use of the scientific methodology of classification, analysis, synthesis, and measurement. The establishment of standards and specifications, the functionalization, and the allocation of responsibility certainly involve the most careful classification. The study of the methods of treating tool steel in order to treble its cutting power requires the most painstaking analysis. Tying processes together by routing work and materials with general orders, special orders, work orders, purchase orders, tickler memoranda, instruction cards, and controlling the whole manufacturing plant by a detailed cost-accounting system, involves the most persistent synthesis. Measurement, too, thoroughgoing and exhaustive, permeates the whole system.[9] For example, in the manufacture of locomotive tires, the system demands that the raw steel, the cutting tools, the arrangements of cutting machinery, the belting, the power load, the lubricating and cooling devices, the handling of supplies, and the physical motions of the men who run the tools, must all be measured as well as analyzed, classified, and synthetized by hundreds of laboratory experiments until the *best* way is found.[10] Time and motion studies, job specifications, and the application of measurement to the process of selecting workers, all are important.

Few, if any, manufacturing plants can be found to-day that are closely modeled after Taylor's system, set up at Bethlehem. Nevertheless, Taylor's influence has been enormous, and scientific methods of management are coming into wider and more general factory use, as well as into more intensive application within the factories using them. "Taylorism" had some of the spiritual elements of a gospel, and some of Taylor's early followers undoubtedly went too far in their adherence to its principles as dogma, and in their insistence that only by complete fundamentalism would manufacturers be saved. Fortunately, business enterprise has recognized that the material elements of Taylor's system are unimportant as compared with his idea of applying scientific methods to changing problems. Charlatanism in the name of scientific management has, of course, persisted; but on the whole, modesty, humility and a truly scientific approach have characterized the efforts of management to control and reduce the costs of manufacturing.

As has already been indicated, most of the progress in the application of science to the problem of controlling and reducing costs has been confined to increasing the effective use of the methods and means of manufacturing. Management has given the majority of its efforts to manufacturing costs and not to total costs. Management has called upon technical experts and trained engineers of every kind. These experts have tackled one machine and improved it; one process, one method. They have time-studied operations, and frequently they have "improved the operators themselves to their pecuniary, mental and physical advantage." [11] By 1914, the standardization of manufacturing methods and the application of scientific management to labor and machinery had built up an amazing productive mechanism. "Unheard-of production capacity, mountains of annual volume, undreamed-of low-unit costs were the factors which made America a nation of almost unparalleled wealth and high wages." [12]

Perhaps the greatest task of management at the moment is the effective control and possible reduction of marketing costs. In many instances the rewards of manufacturing ingenuity have been "swallowed up" by wasteful marketing costs. Many business enterprises are discovering that their marketing costs are steadily increasing and that they have exhausted the major possibilities in reducing their manufacturing costs. Such a condition reflects itself in lower profits and presents to management its next big task. Each part of the marketing fabric needs to be taken apart and gauged, not with hardened steel gauges, perhaps, but with persistent analysis, classification, and measurement. Worn, inadequate, and incompetent timber must be ripped out of the external sales personnel. Needless operations, lost motions, and monkey motions are all too prevalent in personal selling. [13] Similar study and experiment must also be applied to the internal marketing organization. The type of planning and use of advertising described in the following statement must be discarded:

> If a large volume of advertising in a given case fails to do the job, the volume is likely to be increased instead of the character and the mediums being changed and other marketing factors brought into strict coordination, as tho a 100 per cent. job could be done by adding in volume to a 50 per cent. or 75 per cent. content of weakness and paucity of definition, and a considerable degree of indirection.[14]

Surely any such procedure can hardly stand up to scientific test and experimentation with means and methods.

The costs of indirect material, indirect labor, indirect expenses and administrative expenses also need to be controlled and reduced if possible. Management must be concerned with the total costs of its particular business operations. It is definitely interested in pushing lower the purchase price (cost) of its total operations.

Considered in the internal sense and somewhat irrespective of the scale of operations, the task of management rests, then, squarely upon a scientific investigation of facts as the determinant of all action. If Spencer's idea of tragedy was a theory killed by a fact, management's idea of tragedy must be a fact killed by a theory. Broadly speaking, experience in scientific management has already established certain prac-

tises which are based upon facts that appear to
be "general and enduring." These practises,
management can apply internally to the whole
of the business enterprise. They are functional
organization, the separation of planning and detail execution, standardization (of product, of
materials, of equipment and condition of equipment, of methods, of times and rates, and of
personnel), and the establishment of system or
routine.[15]

Our first chapter, it will be recalled, dealt
at some length with the interesting economic
anomaly or conflict between the aims of society
and the aims of business. It was pointed out
that society is concerned with the making of
goods, while the business man is concerned with
the making of money. Our discussion of the task
of management has emphasized its central profit-
making purpose. It is hardly necessary to indicate that in so far as management concerns
itself with developing technical efficiency and
reducing total costs it tends to bring the profit
motive toward an absolute coincidence with social welfare. In spite of management's obvious
oversights and common neglects, in its internal
efforts to secure the greatest economy of material
and efficiency of method, it is making progress
toward the solution of the economic anomaly.
Specifically, its contributions appear to be as
follows: It tends to make possible a larger vol-

ume of production from a given amount of productive equipment; it increases the certainty
and regularity of plant operation by making less
frequent interruptions caused by lack of materials, breakdowns, strikes and lockouts; it tends
to prevent the creation of surplus plant capacity
(particularly when management gives the
proper amount of attention to marketing); and
it brings about a selection of workers in line
with the requirements of particular jobs which
must be done, the training of workers in the
best technique for the job, and the creation of
incentives to greater effort by workers.[16] In these
respects, at least, the necessity for making profits works toward the social welfare, the making of goods.

From the point of view of increasing the efficiency and cutting the costs of all the internal
operations of a business enterprise it is scarcely
surprizing that business management turns toward large-scale operation. Profits depend upon
the volume of transactions as well as upon efficiency. In fact, the present or future volume
of transactions is one of the most important elements in reducing unit-manufacturing costs.
The growth in the size and scope of business
enterprises is very largely caused by management's desire for volume. The pecuniary advantages of large-scale operations as they relate to

total costs are indeed appealing. They may be summarized as follows:

Economies in Manufacturing

1. The materials required—raw, fabricating, installation, accessory, as well as fuel and power —can generally be secured more cheaply when purchased in large quantities.
2. Labor may be more effectively utilized, since processes can be minutely divided.
3. Plant and equipment may be more advantageously utilized. The demand for products may be forecast more accurately and coordinated with the manufacturing program to avoid slack and rush periods of work.
4. The materials may be more effectively utilized, either by manufacturing by-products or by disposing of waste in bulk.
5. Standardization can be more easily applied.
6. Research may be carried on at less per unit of output.

Economies in Marketing

1. Transportation may be carried on in greater bulk, resulting in a saving per unit transported.
2. Advertising costs may be decreased in unit cost altho the total volume may be increased.
3. The personal sales force required will not increase in the ratio in which the sales increase, therefore resulting in less cost per unit of product.
4. Branch selling agencies may be maintained.
5. The value of good-will and of trade-marks will increase with the volume of business.

[197]

Economies in Management

1. The "overhead" cost per unit of product, and in particular the fixed charges, will not increase proportionately to the production.
2. Better management can be secured and afforded.
3. Cost accounting and production control systems can be introduced at less cost per unit of product.

Economies in Finance

1. Borrowings can be effected at cheaper rates as a result of larger issues of bonds and of better security.
2. The amount of risk taken will be less because of the pooling of profits and losses, the greater ability to study outside market conditions, and the more able management.
3. Greater financial resources will be available in case of depression or business strain."

In order to secure any large number of these possible economies which present themselves under large-scale enterprise, management must increase its own efficiency to the nth degree. As business units grow, the importance of total costs becomes of tremendous moment to management. So far as low manufacturing costs are involved, large-scale mass production depends upon a large volume of sales, standardization of product line, and continuity of production. Glutted markets, the desire for variety in style offerings, and hand-to-mouth buying are only a few of the conditions which operate to make continuous and profitable mass production difficult. The choice between an attempt to force sales by intensive and extensive marketing which may be so costly as to offset the savings in mass manufacturing and an attempt to work out a proper correlation between carefully-determined sales possibilities at reasonable sales costs and the schedule of factory output is a fine and hazardous matter of decision. Moreover, there is always the chance that "giant, on-rushing" manufacture may become careless manufacture—or even "antiquated" manufacture. In the long pull, sound quality is probably more profitable than careless quantity.

Moreover, there is the ever-present possibility that the capacity of men to team well may set up a boundary for efficient and economical operation. There are some business philosophers who believe that the "ability of control and management" is the most important limiting factor upon the economy of large business, and that it must be regarded "as a constant factor." [18] Certain it is that management must acquire new and more flexible techniques if the growth of business units is to go on unceasingly.

Once we grant the ability of management to cope with the problems of large-scale operation, it appears that the very growth of business enterprise tends to make it more necessary to make more commodities in order to make more money. The utilization of by-products makes for social welfare, both because of the by-products themselves and because their development, fabrication, and sale contributes profits which may tend to lower the selling prices of the major items in the product line. Again, the integration of processes possible in a large business enterprise reduces those restrictive forces which might otherwise be exercised to limit the production of such an enterprise. When an industrial enterprise is absolutely dependent upon others, say, for materials or power, it is in a precarious position and may be forced to shut down and stop production for a period. Moreover, large-scale business enterprises can better afford to engage in technical and mechanical experimentation and research than can the small-scale enterprise. These investigations may develop better methods of making goods and in this sense large-scale operation contributes "cumulatively to material production." [19]

So far we have stressed the work of management in the direction and execution of the internal operations of the business enterprise. Management, however, must also assume the task of coordinating its business interests with those external conditions which exist outside the enterprise itself. It is plain that every business enterprise is surrounded by a multitude of broad social relationships. Only the most significant need be mentioned here. So far as management is involved, they appear to be the enterprise's relationship with the trade and with the "state."

The trade association generally serves as a central agency for "fostering, furthering, and supervising" the external relationships of competing business enterprises one with another. These associations trace their ancestry back to the medieval craft gilds and the Hanseatic League, but they are vastly different in their interests and significance. There are perhaps some twenty-five thousand of them in the United States to-day. They carry on a wide variety of activities "embracing every conceivable phase of economic interest."

They may collect, compile, prepare, and disseminate statistical data of production, stocks on hand, shipments, or cancellations. They may engage in legislative propaganda and lobbying in the interests of the trade. They may aid in influencing their individual members to adopt simplified practise agreements. They may study cost problems, prepare and distribute standard cost systems to the trade. They may set up a credit-and-collection clearing house for their several members. They may work out codes of trading ethics and encourage their adoption. They may conduct traffic bureaus for the study of rates, classifications, car supplies, and so on. They may organize and operate research departments to study personnel work, accident prevention, distribution costs and any other business problem. They may engage in industrial research and maintain laboratories staffed by technical experts. They may develop cooperative buying associations and reciprocal patent agreements. Most of these activities deserve the support of the management of the individual business enterprise. In their results, most of them facilitate management's pursuit of profits, and at the same time are conducive to larger outputs of goods than would be manufactured without their operation.

Such trade-association activities as may attempt to regulate output by agreement or to fix prices are of another color. In the first place, they are quite definitely illegal, as an increasing amount of judicial opinion will attest.[20] In the second place, such practises do not develop any close or continuing relationships between the profits gained and social welfare. Of course, an agreement between competing managements to restrict output under the auspices of a trade association does not necessarily mean that the "total amount produced by all the parties to the agreement will be any less than it would be if no such agreement existed."[21] Therefore, while agreements to limit production are illegal, and while they are not positively conducive to social welfare, neither are they necessarily and ultimately restrictive of production.

The present attitude of management toward the trade association is not exclusively dominated by the desire to create price differentials which will mean more profits for the individual enterprise at the expense of social welfare. At first, of course, management accepted individual membership in the trade association more or less reluctantly, and with a willingness to receive all it could without giving or conforming in return. It saw in the trade association only such advantages as central credit records, united pressure in securing tariff privileges or united defensive action against restrictive legislation. But that attitude has changed. The importance of cooperative and collaborative efforts are widely recognized by management to-day. In an effort to break away from malicious competition and from excessive individualism "under circumstances which make individualism a bull in a china shop," management is turning to the trade association for the modification of the "destructive elements" in present business practise. As President Hoover has said, "We are, almost unnoticed, in the midst of a great revolution, or perhaps a better word, a transformation in the whole superorganization of our economic life. We are passing from a period of extremely individualistic action into a period of associational activities.''

Much the same change has come about in the attitude of management toward the state. While there is still a deal of legislative ''lobbying,'' paid propaganda of questionable veracity, and while we still hear loud cries about ''less government'' in business, management is becoming more alert to the probabilities of the reaction of society to slippery business practises. Moreover, management is coming to a realization that voluntarily-taken corrective measures enormously build up the public good-will. Voluntary conduct which corrects social inconveniences will thereby remove the particular stimuli to social reaction and resultant legislation. Until management can purge business of its abuses by individual or associative action, it need expect no mercy from the government. There is a growing amount of evidence, however, that management is voluntarily experimenting to these ends in the ever strengthening conviction ''that good-will is after all the *sine qua non* of survival, and that one of the most effective means for the attainment of that good-will is through collaborative effort in building up accepted standards of sound trade ethics.'' [22]